THE LETTERS OF
DOROTHY OSBORNE

The Letters of Dorothy Osborne

Edited by Kingsley Hart

to Sir William Temple 1652-54

The Folio Society 1968

The text of this edition is used by kind permission of
J. M. Dent and Sons Ltd and The Clarendon Press, Oxford

PRINTED IN GREAT BRITAIN

Printed and Bound by W & J Mackay & Co Ltd, Chatham

Contents

Illustrations

The portrait of Sir William Temple by Sir Peter Lely is reproduced by kind permission of the National Portrait Gallery and that of Dorothy Osborne, by an unknown artist, is from the Broadlands Collection.

Introduction

Love-letters are comparatively rare in English literature. Those written by Dorothy Osborne to William Temple between December 1652 and December 1654 are among the few that have established their right to be remembered; ever since some of them were published as a supplement to *Memoirs of the Life, Works, and Correspondence of Sir William Temple, Bart,* by Thomas Courtenay in 1836, an increasingly high place has been accorded them. To-day, they stand with the diaries of Pepys and Evelyn as fascinating personal documents of one of the most eventful periods in our history.

One explanation of the fascination these letters have held for readers, historians, and critics from Macaulay to Virginia Woolf and Lord David Cecil is to be found in the principle of letter-writing followed by Dorothy Osborne herself: *'all letters, methinks, should be free and easy as one's discourse,'* she wrote, and their greatest charm lies in the unselfconscious intimacy and ease with which she penned her thoughts, whether to tease her lover, rail at their misfortunes, describe a dinner party or reveal the secret places of her heart to him. They are, in short, eminently readable. It is with no sense of embarrassment that the reader listens to Dorothy's sincere, honest, and forthright declarations of love, such as this one written to Temple at a time when he was expecting to be sent on a mission to Sweden:

How shall I long when you are gone your journey to hear from you! how I apprehend a thousand accidents that are not likely nor will never happen, I hope! Oh, if you do not send me long letters, then you are the cruellest person that can be! If you love me you will; and if you do not, I shall never love myself.

She concludes this letter with the same disarming simplicity:

Chide me when I do anything that is not well, but then make haste to tell me that you have forgiven me, and that you are what I shall ever be, a faithful friend.

But the quality of Dorothy Osborne's letters does not by any means depend only on their style and the nature of the personal statements they make; they also tell a story. *'Can there be a more romance story than ours would make if the conclusion should prove happy?'* she wrote, and over a period of two years they give as complete an account as one could hope to find of the longing, despair, happiness, and frustration experienced by two young people desperately in love in a period known to most of us only through history books read with some reluctance at school. Like all good stories, the letters have a richly textured background; for all their occasional romantic flights of fancy, Dorothy Osborne and William Temple did not really want to shut out the world in which they lived, nor did they wish to deny the obligation that both of them felt towards it. So the story of their love-affair unfolds itself against an equally fascinating picture of the age in which they lived.

From the tranquillity of her country home in Bedfordshire, Dorothy discusses events of both national and local significance: we hear of Cromwell's dissolution of Parliament in April 1653; Dorothy comments on General Monk's unfortunate marriage and its consequences, and later, writing to Temple in Ireland from London, she tells him that like other travellers she is confined to the City as a result of the discovery of a plot to assassinate the Lord Protector. We also learn a great deal about the kind of life led by the aristocracy and landed gentry during the 1650s, their anxieties, their amusements, and their intrigues. She shows great concern for their moral standards when she writes:

'Tis strange to see the folly that possesses the young people of this age, and the liberties they take to themselves. I have the charity to believe they appear very much worse than they are, and that the want of a Court to govern themselves by is in great part the cause of their ruin.

We normally think of life under Puritan rule as being uniformly grey and joyless, but Dorothy tells us of masques, of race meetings, of gay evenings in New Spring Gardens, and of how

8

she supped and saw a play at the Three Kings. In the country we hear of happy shepherdesses and an idyllic pastoral life, and when Dorothy stayed with her brother-in-law in Kent she was caught up in a social round that she found extremely exhausting. We meet, too, some of the most characteristic personalities of the age who generally figure little in history books. There is Sir Thomas de Mayerne, a fashionable physician; Peter Lely, the portrait painter; William Lilly, the astrologer, and in Dorothy's opinion an inadequate fortune-teller; Stephen Marshall, a popular preacher; the eccentric Lady Newcastle, and hosts of others. But the most interesting aspect of the many personalities and relationships that Dorothy mentions is that new light is thrown on their involvement in the crucial conflicts of the day, and the generalizations of history books concerning the conflicting loyalties that appeared among members of the same family acquire a sharper focus. A closer look at the Osborne and Temple families shows this: Temple's uncle, Dr Henry Hammond, was a staunch supporter of the Royalist cause; Sir John Temple, William's father, sat in the Long Parliament and held an office in Ireland under Cromwell to which he had been appointed by Charles I; William's cousin had served Cromwell as a soldier. Dorothy's father and brother were ardent Royalists, but her uncle, Sir John Danvers, was a regicide. There is, however, no evidence of any breach in family relations as a result of these different political sympathies: Sir John Danvers seems to have been on good terms with his Royalist sister Lady Gargrave, with whom Dorothy often stayed in London, and even with Sir Peter Osborne, Dorothy's father. After they were married, Dorothy and William stayed for a while in complete harmony with his Puritan relations at Reading. But perhaps most important of all is the fact that at no time between 1651 and 1654, when so many objections were raised to an alliance between Dorothy and William, were political sympathies mentioned as being of any significance. On the contrary, the Protector's son, Henry Cromwell, was at one time considered by her family as an extremely eligible suitor.

The 'Romance Story' of William and Dorothy began in 1648. She was twenty-one at the time and he was a year younger. Dorothy and her brother were on their way to join their father at St Malo, where, as Lieutenant-Governor of Guernsey, Sir Peter Osborne was gallantly trying to provide for the starving garrison on the island, which he was holding for the King. They broke their journey on the Isle of Wight, where the King was imprisoned at Carisbrooke Castle. There Dorothy and William met. He joined the party and accompanied them to St Malo. He was bound for Paris, but stayed for some time at St Malo, where we can assume that their love blossomed. Word of this reached Sir John Temple, who in no uncertain manner instructed his son to proceed to Paris forthwith. It must have been a hard blow for Dorothy to be separated from him so soon. Writing early in 1654 to Temple, she recalled the year in France with her father and the change it effected in her, which must have been due in part to this separation:

When I came out of France, nobody knew me again. I was so altered, from a cheerful humour that was always alike, never over merry but always pleased, I was grown heavy and sullen, froward and discomposed; and that country which usually gives people a jolliness and gaiety that is natural to the climate, had wrought in me so contrary effects that I was as new a thing to them as my clothes.

Sir Peter and Dorothy returned to England in the summer of 1649. He was immediately engaged in the settling of his own affairs: the payment of a fine upon his estate, which had been sequestrated by the Roundheads during his absence. He then retired with his family to his ancestral home, Chicksands in Bedfordshire, in sadly reduced circumstances. Temple returned to London during the winter of 1650–1651. Dorothy was staying with relations for part of that time and the lovers were reunited. Again, Sir John Temple felt that his son was being distracted from making a career for himself, and summoned him to York, from where William was sent to the Continent. Back at Chicksands, Dorothy heard little from Temple until his return to London in the late autumn of 1652, when the correspondence that forms the material of this book was started.

During Temple's absence on the Continent, Dorothy was subjected to many attempts by her family to find a suitable husband for her. They knew, of course, of her feelings for Temple and disapproved of them. Dorothy must have a richer husband, and one with greater prospects of a brilliant career. William's father adopted a comparable attitude towards Dorothy: his son should marry a woman with a more substantial fortune. The early letters from Dorothy to William contain much that illuminates this situation: Dorothy is most anxious to win Sir John's favour, and we learn of her family's search for a suitable husband.

Throughout the correspondence Dorothy reveals consistent and characteristic attitudes to her love for Temple, her loyalty to her family, and to the subject of marriage in general. She is always realistic about the prospects of a happy outcome for them:

I cannot promise that I shall be yours because I know not how far my misfortunes may reach, nor what punishments are reserved for my fault, but I dare almost promise you shall never receive the displeasure of seeing me another's.

Sometimes her realistc approach is combined with a witty playfulness towards her suitors, and towards Temple himself:

Just now I have news brought me of the death of an old rich knight that has promised me this seven years to marry me whensoever his wife died, and now he's dead before her, and has left her such a widow, it makes me mad to think on't, £1,200 a year jointure and £20,000 in money and personal estate, and all this I might have had if Mr. Death had been pleased to have taken her instead of him. Well, who can help these things? But, since I cannot have him, would you have her! What say you? Shall I speak a good word for you?

She is very forthright about the sense of duty and loyalty she feels towards her family, particularly to her father:

I can never think of disposing myself without my father's consent; and though he has left it more in my power than almost anybody leaves a daughter, yet certainly I were the worst natured person in the world if his kindness were not a greater tie upon me than any advantage he could have reserved. Besides that, 'tis my duty, from which nothing can ever tempt me, nor could you like it in me if I should do otherwise, 'twould make me unworthy in your esteem.

11

At times she is equally forthright, even sharp, with Temple himself. On one occasion when he misunderstood something she had said she wrote:

I shall take heed though hereafter what I write, since you are so good at raising doubts to persecute yourself withal, and shall condemn my own easy faith no more; for sure 'tis a better-natured and a less fault to believe too much than to distrust where there is no cause.

After discussing some recent scandal or the proposed marriage of an acquaintance, her comments on marriage in general reveal her characteristically realistic approach to life:

What an age we do live in, where 'tis a miracle if in ten couple that are married, two of them live so as not to publish to the world that they cannot agree.

or:

'Tis much easier, sure, to get a good fortune than a good husband.

Her own recipe for a happy marriage is very simply stated: '*if we are friends we must both obey and command alike*', and throughout the long period of waiting and hoping for some resolution of their problems her conviction that William Temple was the man for her only faltered once. At the end of 1653, worn down by endless arguments on the subject of love and marriage with her strangely possessive brother Henry, and exhausted by the nervous frustration of a brief and unsatisfactory reunion with Temple in London, she succumbed to the natural tendency to melancholy that had threatened to ruin her health and peace of mind before. She wrote offering to release Temple from his obligation to her and suggested he should marry someone else. Always a deeply religious person, Dorothy took refuge in her faith, and begged Temple to conquer a passion that threatened to destroy him:

I tremble at the desperate things you say in your letter; for the love of God, consider seriously with yourself what can enter into comparison with the safety of your soul. Are a thousand women, or ten thousand worlds, worth it? No, you cannot have so little reason left as you pretend, nor so little religion. For God's sake let us not neglect what can only make us happy for a trifle. If God had seen it fit to have satisfied our desires we should have had them, and everything would not have conspired thus to cross them. Since He has decreed it otherwise we must submit, and not by striving make an innocent passion a sin, and show a childish stubbornness.

But Temple would not accept this. Before leaving for Ireland to join his father, he visited Dorothy at Chicksands. The letters written after this visit show that he succeeded in dispelling her melancholy fears, and that both of them were resolved to wait with patience for the gradual weakening of family resistance. Sir Peter Osborne died in March 1654, and Dorothy immediately insisted that her engagement to Temple be made public. By June the long and formal negotiations connected with the marriage settlement had begun. Their love had triumphed. It was bound to, for they had a talent for what Dorothy described as *'perfect friendship'* that demanded general acceptance even though it was not understood. This talent, she said, *'is not to be taught, it must come naturally to those who have it, and those who have it not can ne'er be made to understand it.'*

Temple kept his wife's love-letters after his marriage, and they remained in the family until 1891, when the bulk of them were sold to the British Museum. The first edition of the letters appeared in 1888, edited by Judge Parry, whose interest in Dorothy Osborne had been aroused by Macaulay's review of Courtenay's *Life* of Temple in 1838. In 1903 a revised and extended edition appeared, later published by Dent in both the *Wayfarer's Library* and *Everyman's Library* in 1914. Today, the definitive edition is that of G. C. Moore Smith, published by the Oxford University Press in 1928, incorporating additional letters, and extracts from the Diary of Henry Osborne. The present edition is based on the work of both Parry and Moore Smith, to whom all those interested in Dorothy Osborne owe an inestimable debt of gratitude. The text used here is substantially that of Parry's *Everyman* edition, but the dating and order of the letters are Moore Smith's, whose notes and comments have been extensively resorted to.

The Letters of Dorothy Osborne

TO SIR WILLIAM TEMPLE

1652–1654

Letter 1

Temple left England on an extended Continental journey, probably during the summer of 1651. He had warned Dorothy that she might not hear from him for some weeks, and as the months went by she began to think that he had decided to travel further. Sometime in March 1652 she received a letter from him from Breda. Then another long silence ensued, leading her to suppose that he had gone to Italy. Now she is overjoyed to hear that he has returned to England.

'My old servant' is undoubtedly Temple himself, and the 'ten pounds he claimed' a reference to a lovers' wager between them regarding her constancy. This is Dorothy's playful way of pointing out that she has remained constant during the period of silence between them. There is a further reference to this wager in Letter 35.

DECEMBER THE 24TH [1652]

SIR, You may please to let my old servant (as you call him) know that I confess I owe much to his merits and the many obligations his kindness and civilities has laid upon me; but for the ten pound he claims, it is not yet due, and I think you may do well to persuade him (as a friend) to put it in the number of his desperate debts, for 'tis a very uncertain one. In all things else, pray say I am his servant. And now, sir, let me tell you that I am extremely glad (whosoever gave you the occasion) to hear from you, since (without compliment) there are very few persons in the world I am more concerned in. To find that you have overcome your long journey, that you are well and in a place where it is possible for me to see you, is such a satisfaction as I, who have not been used to many, may be allowed to doubt of. Yet I will hope my eyes do not deceive me, and that I have not forgot to read; but if you please to confirm it to me by another, you know how to direct it, for I am where I was, still the same, and always

Your humble servant,
D. Osborne

FOR MRS. PAINTER,
IN COVENT GARDEN.
(Keep this letter till it be called for.)

Letter 2

Dorothy refers to incidents that had occurred during the summer of 1651, before Temple's departure for the Continent. He had passed through Bedford on his way north to join his father in York. She chides him for not coming to see her and for staying abroad much longer than she expected.

JANUARY THE 2ND, 1653*

SIR, If there were anything in my letter that pleased you I am extremely glad on't, 'twas all due to you, and made it but an equal return for the satisfaction yours gave me. And whatsoever you may believe, I shall never repent the good opinion I have with so much reason taken up. But I forget myself; I meant to chide, and I think this is nothing towards it. Is it possible you came so near me as Bedford and would not see me? Seriously, I should not have believed it from another; would your horse had lost all his legs instead of a hoof, that he might not have been able to carry you further, and you, something that you valued extremely, and could not hope to find anywhere but at Chicksands. I could wish you a thousand little mischances, I am so angry with you; for my life I could not imagine how I had lost you, or why you should call that a silence of six or eight weeks which you intended so much longer. And when I had wearied myself with thinking of all the unpleasant accidents that might cause it, I at length sat down with a resolution to choose the best to believe, which was that at the end of one journey you had begun another (which I had heard you say you intended), and that your haste, or something else, had hindered you from letting me know it. In this ignorance your letter from Breda found me, which, by the way, Sir Thomas† never saw. 'Tis true I told him I had a letter from

* This letter is dated 'Jan yᵉ 2d 1652'. According to the reckoning of the time, New Year's Day fell on March 25th. Throughout this edition dates have been brought into line with the modern calendar.

† Sir Thomas Osborne, Dorothy's cousin on her mother's side. Although he was three or four years Dorothy's junior, it seems clear from Henry Osborne's diary that attempts had been made to arrange a marriage between them. Later he became Earl of Danby and Duke of Leeds and a prominent figure in political life.

you, one day that he extremely lamented he knew not what was become of you, and fell into so earnest commendations of you that I cannot expect less from him who have the honour to be his kinswoman. But to leave him to his mistress who perhaps has spoilt his memory—let me assure you that I was never so in love with an old man in my life, as I was with Mr. Metcalf for sending me that letter (though there is one not far off that says he will have me when his wife dies).* I writ so kindly to him the next post, and he that would not be in my debt sends me word again that you were coming over. But yours kept me from believing that and made me think you in Italy when you were in England, though I was not displeased to find myself deceived. But for God sake let me ask you what you have done all this while you have been away; what you have met with in Holland that could keep you there so long; why you went no further; and why I was not to know you went so far? You may do well to satisfy me in all these. I shall so persecute you with questions else, when I see you, that you will be glad to go thither again to avoid me; though when that will be I cannot certainly say, for my father has so small a proportion of health left him since my mother's death, that I am in continual fear of him, and dare not often make use of the leave he gives me to be from home, lest he should at some time want such little services as I am able to render him. Yet I think to be in London in the next term,† and am sure I shall desire it because you are there.

Sir, your humble servant.

Letter 3

Dorothy begins her account of her life since their last meeting (and parting) at Goring House during the winter of 1650–1651. Goring House, the London residence of the Earl of Norwich, was on the site of the present Buckingham Palace.

* Sir William Briers, whose death is mentioned in Letter 23.

† It was common practice at the time for people not directly concerned with the Law to visit London during the 'terms' or periods when the Law Courts were open.

She has spent most of this time at Chicksands in Bedfordshire, the Osborne family home, with occasional visits to London. She mentions a visit to her maternal aunt, Lady Gargrave, and reveals the anxiety of the whole family, particularly of her brother Henry, to arrange a suitable marriage for her. It is not possible to identify all Dorothy's suitors with any certainty, but some mentioned here are referred to in later letters, notably 'the widower that had four daughters'. He was Sir Justinian Isham, later called by Dorothy 'the Emperor' and further described by her in Letter 4.

The state of low spirits and nervous depression to which she gives the fashionable name of 'the spleen' was undoubtedly aggravated by Temple's absence and long silence. Henry Osborne's diary reveals that it was to Epsom that she went to take the waters.

[SATURDAY JANUARY THE 8TH, 1653]

SIR, There is nothing moves my charity like gratitude; and when a beggar's thankful for a small relief, I always repent it was not more. But seriously, this place will not afford much towards the enlarging of a letter, and I am grown so dull with living in't (for I am not willing to confess that I was always so) as to need all helps. Yet you shall see I will endeavour to satisfy you, upon condition you will tell me why you quarrelled so at your last letter. I cannot guess at it, unless it were that you repented you told me so much of your story, which I am not apt to believe neither, because it would not become our friendship, a great part of it consisting (as I have been taught) in a mutual confidence. And to let you see that I believe it so, I will give you an account of myself, and begin my story, as you did yours, from our parting at Goring House.

I came down hither not half so well pleased as I went up, with an engagement upon me that I had little hope of ever shaking off, for I had made use of all the liberty my friends would allow me to preserve my own, and 'twould not do; he was so weary of his, that he would part with't upon my terms. As my last refuge I got my brother to go down with him to see his house, who, when he came back, made the relation I wished. He said the seat was as ill as so good a country would permit, and the house so ruined for want of living in't, as it would ask a good proportion of time and money to make it fit for a woman to confine herself to. This (though it were not much) I was willing to take hold of, and made it considerable enough to break the engagement. I had no quarrel to his person or his fortune, but was in love with neither, and much out of love with a thing called marriage; and have since thanked God I was so, for 'tis not long since one of my brothers writ me word of him that he was killed in a duel, though since I hear that 'twas the other that was killed, and he is fled upon 't, which does not mend the matter much. Both made me glad I had 'scaped him, and sorry for his misfortune, which in earnest was the least return his many civilities to me could deserve.

Presently, after this was at an end, my mother died, and I was left at liberty to mourn her loss awhile. At length my aunt (with whom I was when you last saw me) commanded me to wait on her at London; and when I came she told me how much I was in her care, how well she loved me for my mother's sake, and something for my own, and drew out a long set speech which ended in a good motion (as she called it); and truly I saw no harm in't, for by what I had heard of the gentleman I guessed he expected a better fortune than mine. And it proved so. Yet he protested he liked me so well, that he was very angry my father would not be persuaded to give a £1,000 more with me; and I him so ill, that I vowed if I had £1,000 less I should have thought it too much for him. And so we parted. Since, he has made a story with a new mistress that is worth your knowing, but too long for a letter. I'll keep it for you.

After this, some friends that had observed a gravity in my face which might become an elderly man's wife (as they term'd it) and a mother-in-law, proposed a widower to me, that had four daughters, all old enough to be my sisters; but he had a great estate, was as fine a gentleman as ever England bred, and the very pattern of wisdom. I that knew how much I wanted it, thought this the safest place for me to engage in, and was mightily pleased to think I had met with one at last that had wit enough for himself and me too. But shall I tell you what I thought when I knew him (you will say nothing on't): 'twas the vainest, impertinent, self-conceited learned coxcomb that ever yet I saw; to say more were to spoil his marriage, which I hear he is towards with a daughter of my Lord of Coleraine's; but for his sake I shall take heed of a fine gentleman as long as I live.

Before I had quite ended with him, coming to town about that and some other occasions of my own, I fell in Sir Thomas's way; and what humour took him I cannot imagine, but he made very formal addresses to me, and engaged his mother and my brother to appear in't. This bred a story pleasanter than any I have told you yet, but so long a one that I must reserve it till we meet, or make it a letter of itself. Only by this you may see 'twas not for nothing he commended me, though to speak seriously, it was because it was to you. Otherwise I might have missed of his praises for we have hardly been cousins since the breaking up of that business.

The next thing I desired to be rid on was a scurvy spleen that I had ever been subject to, and to that purpose was advised to drink the waters. There I spent the latter end of the summer, and at my coming home found that a gentleman (who has some estate in this country) had been treating with my brother, and it yet goes on fair and softly. I do not know him so well as to give you much of his character: 'tis a modest, melancholy, reserved man, whose head is so taken up with little philosophical studies, that I admire how I found a room there. 'Twas sure by chance; and unless he is pleased with that part of my humour which other people think worst, 'tis very possible the next new experiment may crowd me out again. Thus you have all my late adventures, and almost as much as this paper will hold. The rest shall be employed in telling you how sorry I am you have got such a cold. I am the more sensible of your trouble by my own, for I have newly got one myself. But I will send you that which used to cure me. 'Tis like the rest of my medicines: if it do no good, 'twill be sure to do no harm, and 'twill be no great trouble to you to eat a little on't now and then; for the taste, as it is not excellent, so 'tis not very ill. One thing more I must tell you, which is that you are not to take it ill that I mistook your age by my computation of your journey through this country; for I was persuaded t'other day that I could not be less than thirty years

old by one that believed it himself, because he was sure it was a
great while since he had heard of such a one in the world

As your humble servant.

Letter 4

*Dorothy continues her playful account of Sir Justinian Isham, saying that
if she were to marry Isham she would see that Temple married one of
her stepdaughters. She goes on to express her strong views on marriage
without affection.*

*Her mention of 'disorders at your masques' is of special interest:
masques and other entertainments, although frowned on by the Puritans,
were by no means uncommon during the Commonwealth regime.*

[SATURDAY JANUARY THE 15TH, 1653]

SIR, Since you are so easy to please, sure I shall not miss it, and
if my idle thoughts and dreams will satisfy you, I am to blame if
you want long letters. To begin this, let me tell you I had not
forgot you in your absence. I always meant you one of my
daughters. You should have had your choice, and, trust me, they
say some of them are handsome; but since things did not succeed,
I thought to have said nothing on't, lest you should imagine I
expected thanks for my good intention, or rather lest you should
be too much affected with the thought of what you have lost by
my imprudence. It would have been a good strengthening to my
Party (as you say); but, in earnest, that was not it I aimed at, I
only desired to have it in my power to oblige you; and 'tis certain
I had proved a most excellent mother-in-law. Oh, my conscience!
we should all have joined against him as the common enemy, for
those poor young wenches are as weary of his government as I
could have been. He gives them such precepts, as they say my
Lord of Dorchester* gives his wife, and keeps them so much

* Henry Pierrepoint, first Marquis of Dorchester, an active Royalist.
After the war he studied Law and Medicine, became a Fellow of the
College of Physicians and joined Gray's Inn. He is mentioned in Letter 64
as one suspected of participation in a Royalist plot against Cromwell.

23

prisoners to a vile house he has in Northamptonshire, that if once I had but let them loose, they and his learning would have been sufficient to have made him mad without my help; but his good fortune would have it otherwise, to which I'll leave him, and proceed to give you some reasons why the other kind motion* was not accepted on. The truth is, I had not that longing to ask a mother-in-law's blessing which you say you should have had, for I knew mine too well to think she could make a good one; besides, I was not so certain of his nature as not to doubt whether she might not corrupt it, nor so confident of his kindness as to assure myself it would last longer than other people's of his age and humour. I am sorry to hear he looks ill, though I think there is no great danger of him. 'Tis but a fit of an ague he has got, that the next charm cures, yet he will be apt to fall into it again upon a new occasion, and one knows not how it may work upon his thin body if it comes too often; it spoiled his beauty, sure, before I knew him, for I could never see it, or else (which is as likely) I do not know it when I see it; besides that, I never look for it in men. It was nothing that I expected made me refuse these, but something that I feared; and, seriously, I find I want courage to marry where I do not like. If we should once come to disputes I know who would have the worst on't, and I have not faith enough to believe a doctrine that is often preached, which is, that though at first one has no kindness for *them*, yet it will grow strangely after marriage. Let them trust to it that think good; for my part, I am clearly of opinion (and shall die in't), that, as the more one sees and knows a person that one likes, one has still the more kindness for them, so, on the other side, one is but the more weary of, and the more averse to, an unpleasant humour for having it perpetually by one. And though I easily believe that to marry one for whom we have already some affection will infinitely increase that kindness, yet I shall never be persuaded that marriage has a charm to raise love out of nothing, much less out of dislike.

This is next to telling you what I dream and when I rise, but you have promised to be content with it. I would now, if I could,

* The suggested marriage to Sir Thomas Osborne (see Letter 2). Osborne had had smallpox in April 1652. He and Temple were friends, particularly later in Temple's career.

tell you when I shall be in town, but I am engaged to my Lady Diana Rich,* my Lord of Holland's daughter (who lies at a gentlewoman's hard by me for sore eyes), that I will not leave the country till she does. She is so much a stranger here, and finds so little company, that she is glad of mine till her eyes will give her leave to look out better. They are mending, and she hopes to be at London before the end of this next term; and so do I, though I shall make but a short stay, for all my business there is at an end when I have seen you, and told you my stories. And, indeed, my brother is so perpetually from home, that I can be very little, unless I would leave my father altogether alone, which would not be well. We hear of great disorders at your masks, but no particulars, only they say the Spanish gravity was much discomposed. I shall expect the relation from you at your best leisure, and pray give me an account how my medicine agrees with your cold. This if you can read it, for 'tis strangely scribbled, will be enough to answer yours, which is not very long this week; and I am grown so provident that I will not lay out more than I receive, but I am very just withal, and therefore you know how to make mine longer when you please; though, to speak truth, if I should make this so, you would hardly have it this week, for 'tis a good while since 'twas called for.

Your humble servant.

Letter 5

Dorothy describes a dream she has had. She gives her further views on marriage and expresses concern for Temple's health.

JANUARY THE 22ND [1653]

SIR, Not to confirm you in your belief of dreams, but to avoid your reproaches, I will tell you a pleasant one of mine. The night before I received your first letter,† I dreamt one brought me a

* One of Dorothy's greatest friends. She is referred to in many of the letters, generally as 'My lady', and always with affection and esteem.

† Temple's letter written in December 1652, to which Letter 1 is the answer.

packet, and told me 'twas from you. I, that remembered you were by your own appointment to be in Italy at that time, asked the messenger where he had it, who told me my lady, your mother, sent him with it to me; there my memory failed me a little, for I forgot you had told me she was dead, and meant to give her many humble thanks if ever I were so happy as to see her. When I had opened the letter I found in it two rings; one was, as I remember, an emerald doublet, but broken in the carriage, I suppose, as it might well be, coming so far; t'other was plain gold, with the longest and the strangest posy that ever was; half on't was Italian, which for my life I could not guess at, though I spent much time about it; the rest was '*there was a Marriage in Cana of Galilee*,' which, though it was Scripture, I had not that reverence for it in my sleep that I should have had, I think, if I had been awake; for in earnest the oddness on't put me into that violent laughing that I waked myself with it; and as a just punishment upon me from that hour to this I could never learn whom those rings were for, nor what was in the letter besides. This is but as extravagant as yours, for 'tis as likely that your mother should send me letters as that I should make a journey to see poor people hanged, or that your teeth should drop out at this age. And now I am out of your dreaming debt let me be bold to tell you, I believe you have been with Lilly* yourself. Nothing but he could tell you my knight's strange name.† I'll swear I could never re-member it when I was not concerned in't, and when people asked it me and were not satisfied with truth (for they took my ignor-ance of a desire to conceal him), I was fain to make names for him, and so instead of one odd servant I had gotten twenty. But, in earnest now, where have you fished him out, for I think he is as little known in the world as I could have wished he should have been if I had married him.

I am sorry you are not satisfied with my exceptions to your friend.‡ I spake in general terms of him and was willing to spare him as much as I could, but everybody is allowed to defend them-

---

* William Lilly, the astrologer. In Letter 72 Dorothy mentions a visit she paid to him.
    † Sir Justinian Isham (see Letters 3 and 4).
    ‡ Sir Thomas Osborne (see Letters 2 and 4).

selves. You may remember a quality that you discovered in him when he told you the story of his being at St. Malo, and in earnest he gave me so many testimonies that it was natural to him, as I could not hope he would ever leave it, and consequently could not believe anything he ever had or should say. If this be not enough I can tell you more hereafter.

And to remove the opinion you have of my niceness, or being hard to please, let me assure you I am so far from desiring my husband should be fond of me at threescore, that I would not have him so at all. 'Tis true I should be glad to have him always kind, and know no reason why he should be wearier of being my master, than he was of being my servant. But it is very possible I may talk ignorantly of marriage; when I come to make sad experiments on it in my own person I shall know more, and say less, for fear of disheartening others (since 'tis no advantage to foreknow a misfortune that cannot be avoided), and for fear of being pitied, which of all things I hate. Lest you should be of the same humour I will not pity you, as lame★ as you are; and to speak truth, if you did like it, you should not have it, for you do not deserve it. Would any one in the world, but you, make such haste for a new cold before the old had left him: in a year, too, when mere colds kill as many as a plague used to do? Well, seriously, either resolve to have more care of yourself, or I renounce my friendship; and as a certain king† (that my learned knight is very well acquainted with), who, seeing one of his confederates in so happy a condition as it was not likely to last, sent his ambassador presently to break off the league betwixt them, lest he should be obliged to mourn the change of his fortune if he continued his friend; so I, with a great deal more reason, do declare that I will no longer be a friend to one that's none to himself, nor apprehend the loss of what you hazard every day at tennis. They had served you well enough if they had crammed a dozen ounces of that precious medicine down your throat to have made you remember a quinzy.

But I have done, and am now at leisure to tell you that it is

★ Sick.
† The story, told by Herodotus, of Amasis, king of Egypt, and Polycrates of Samos.

that daughter of my Lord of Holland (who makes, as you say, so many sore eyes with looking on her) that is here; and if I know her at all, or have any judgment, her beauty is the least of her excellences. And now I speak of her, she has given me the occasion to make a request to you; it will come very seasonably after my chiding, and I have great reason to expect you should be in the humour of doing anything for me. She says that seals are much in fashion, and by showing me some that she has, has set me a-longing for some too; such as are oldest and oddest are most prized, and if you know anybody that is lately come out of Italy, 'tis ten to one but they have store, for they are very common there. I do remember you once sealed a letter to me with as fine a one as I have seen. It was a Neptune, I think, riding upon a dolphin; but I'm afraid it was not yours, for I saw it no more. Any old Roman head is a present for a prince. If such things come in your way, pray remember me. I am sorry my new carrier makes you rise so early, 'tis not good for your cold; how might we do that you might lie a-bed and yet I have your letter? You must use to write before he comes, I think, that it may be sure to be ready against he goes. In earnest consider on't, and take some course that your health and my letters may be both secured, for the loss of either would be very sensible to

Your humble.

Letter 6

In her biography of Temple, Lady Giffard mentions his susceptibility to fits of depression and melancholy. In this letter Dorothy says she has tried to put Temple out of his 'dumps': she makes a strong avowal of her feelings for him and expresses her concern for his future employment abroad. Temple has obviously replied to her request in Letter 5 for seals by saying that if he were a Roman emperor she should have his head.

[SATURDAY JANUARY THE 29TH, 1653]

SIR, I am so great a lover of my bed myself that I can easily apprehend the trouble of rising at four o'clock these cold mornings. In earnest, I am troubled that you should be put to it, and

28

have chid the carrier for coming out so soon; he swears to me he never comes out of town before eleven o'clock, and that my Lady Painter's footman (as he calls him) brings her letters two hours sooner than he needs to do. I told him he was gone one day before the letter came; he vows he was not, and that your old friend Collins never brought letters of my Lady Painter's in 's life; and, to speak truth, Collins did not bring me that letter. I had it from this Harrold two hours before Collins came. Yet it is possible all that he says may not be so, for I have known better men than he lie; therefore if Collins be more for your ease or conveniency, make use of him hereafter. I know not whether my letter were kind or not, but I'll swear yours was not, and am sure mine was meant to be so. It is not kind in you to desire an increase of my friendship; that is to doubt it is not as great already as it can be, than which you cannot do me a greater injury. 'Tis my misfortune indeed that it lies not in my power to give you better testimony on't than words, otherwise I should soon convince you that 'tis the best quality I have, and that where I own a friendship, I mean so perfect a one, as time can neither lessen nor increase. If I said nothing of my coming to town, 'twas because I had nothing to say that I thought you would like to hear. The truth is twenty little cross accidents had made it so uncertain as I was more out of humour with them than you could be with the bells. Though I had no reason to expect otherwise, for I do not know that ever I desired anything earnestly in my life, but 'twas denied me, and I am many times afraid to wish a thing merely lest my Fortune should take that occasion to use me ill. She cannot see, and therefore I may venture to write that I intend to be at London if it be possible on Friday or Saturday come sennight. Be sure you do not read it aloud, lest she hear it, and prevent me, or drive you away before I come. It is so like my luck, too, that you should be going I know not whither again; but trust me, I have looked for't ever since I heard you were come home. You will laugh, sure, when I shall tell you that hearing my Lord Lisle* was to go ambassador

* Dorothy fears that Temple may be sent to Sweden under Lord Lisle, and reminds him of their earlier separation. Philip, Lord Lisle was the eldest son of Robert Sidney, nephew of Sir Philip Sidney. Temple's grandfather had accompanied Sir Philip to the Low Countries in 1585. The

into Sweden, I remember'd your father's acquaintance in that family with an apprehension that he might be in the humour of sending you with him. But for God sake whither is it that you go? I would not willingly be at such a loss again as I was after your Yorkshire journey. If it prove as long a one, I shall not forget you; but in earnest I shall be so possessed with a strong splenetic fancy that I shall never see you more in this world, as all the waters in England* will not cure. Well, this is a sad story; we'll have no more on't.

I humbly thank you for your offer of your head; but if you were an emperor, I should not be so bold with you as to claim your promise; you might find twenty better employments for't. Only with your gracious leave, I think I should be a little exalted with remembering that you had been once my friend; 'twould more endanger my growing proud than being Sir Justinian's mistress, and yet he thought me pretty well inclin'd to't then. Lord! what would I give that I had a Latin letter of his for you, that he writ to a great friend at Oxford, where he gives him a long and learned character of me; 'twould serve you to laugh at this seven year. If I remember what was told me on't, the worst of my faults was a height (he would not call it pride) that was, as he had heard, the humour of my family; and the best of my commendations was, that I was capable of being company and conversation for him. But you do not tell me yet how you found him out. If I had gone about to have concealed him, I had been sweetly served. I shall take heed of you hereafter; because there is no very great likelihood of your being an emperor, or that, if you were, I should have your head.

I have sent into Italy for seals; 'tis to be hoped by that time mine come over, they may be out of fashion again, for 'tis an humour that your old acquaintance Mr. Smith and his lady† has

* During Temple's absence abroad, Dorothy had taken the waters at Epsom Wells (see Letter 3).

† Robert Smith of Bounds Park, Tonbridge. He had married the widowed Countess of Sutherland (*née* Dorothy Sidney) after an unsuccessful courtship of Lady Isabella Blount, who then married the Earl of Banbury.

idea of serving under Lord Lisle was distasteful to Dorothy as she disapproved of his republican opinions.

brought up; they say she wears twenty strung upon a ribbon, like the nuts boys play withal, and I do not hear of anything else. Mr. Howard* presented his mistress but a dozen such seals as are not to be valued as times now go. But *à propos de* Mons. Smith, what a scape has he made of my Lady Banbury; and who would ere have dreamt he should have had my Lady Sunderland, though he be a very fine gentleman, and does more than deserve her. I think I shall never forgive her one thing she said of him, which was that she married him out of pity; it was the pitifullest saying that ever I heard, and made him so contemptible that I should not have married him for that very reason. This is a strange letter, sure, I have not time to read it over, but I have said any-thing that came in my head to put you out of your dumps. For God sake be in better humour, and assure yourself I am as much as you can wish,

Your faithful friend and servant.

Letter 7

Temple has sent Dorothy the seals for which she had asked. She denies any knowledge of a story he has told her concerning Lady Diana Rich.

She looks forward to her visit to London, where she will arrive a few days after writing this letter.

[SATURDAY FEBRUARY THE 5TH, 1653]

SIR, You have made me so rich as I am able to help my neigh-bours. There is a little head cut in an onyx that I take to be a very good one, and the dolphin is (as you say) the better for being cut less; the oddness of the figure makes the beauty of these things. If you saw one that my brother sent my Lady Diana last week, you would believe it were meant to fright people withal; 'twas brought out of the Indies, and cut there for an idol's head: they took the devil himself, sure, for their pattern that did it, for in my life I never saw so ugly a thing, and yet she is as fond on't as if it were as lovely as she herself is. Her eyes

* See Letter 7, note.

have not the flames they have had, nor is she like (I am afraid) to recover them here; but were they irrecoverably lost, the beauty of her mind were enough to make her outshine everybody else, and she would still be courted by all that knew how to value her, like *la belle aveugle* that was Philip the 2nd of France his mistress. I am wholly ignorant of the story you mention, and am confident you are not well informed, for 'tis impossible she should ever have done anything that were unhandsome. If I knew who the person were that is concern'd in't, she allows me so much freedom with her, that I could easily put her upon the discourse, and I do not think she would use much of disguise in it towards me. I should have guessed it Algernon Sydney,* but that I cannot see in him that likelihood of a fortune which you seem to imply by saying 'tis not present. But if you should mean by that, that 'tis possible his wit and good parts may raise him to one, you must pardon if I am not of your opinion, for I do not think these are times for anybody to expect preferment in't, that deserves it, and in the best 'twas ever too uncertain for a wise body to trust to. But I am altogether of your mind, that my Lady Sunderland is not to be followed in her marrying fashion, and that Mr. Smith never appeared less her servant than in desiring it; to speak truth, 'twas convenient for neither of them, and in meaner people had been plain undoing one another, which I cannot understand to be kindness of either side. She has lost by it much of the repute she had gained by keeping herself a widow; it was then believed that wit and discretion were to be reconciled in her person that have so seldom been persuaded to meet in anybody else. But we are all mortal.

I did not mean that Howard. 'Twas Arundel Howard.† And the seals were some remainders that showed his father's love to antiquities, and therefore cost him dear enough if that would make them good. I am sorry I cannot follow your counsel in keeping fair with Fortune. I am not apt to suspect without just

* Second son of Robert, Earl of Leicester. He fought for Cromwell and in 1651 became a member of the Council of State.

† Henry, second son of the Earl of Arundel, collector of the Arundel marbles. Dorothy calls him 'Arundel' Howard in order to distinguish him from the Howard Temple took her reference to mean.

cause, but in earnest if I once find anybody faulty towards me, they lose me for ever; I have forsworn being twice deceived by the same person. For God sake do not say she has the spleen, I shall hate it worse than ever I did, nor that 'tis a disease of the wits, I shall think you abuse me, for then I am sure it would not be mine; but were it certain that they went together always, I dare swear there is nobody so proud of their wit as to keep it upon such terms, but would be glad after they had endured it a while to let them both go as they came. I know nothing yet that is likely to alter my resolution of being in town on Saturday next; but I am uncertain where I shall be, and therefore it will be best that I send you word when I am here. I should be glad to see you sooner, but that I do not know myself what company I may have with me. I meant this letter longer when I began it, but an extreme cold that I have taken lies so in my head, and makes it ache so violently, that I hardly see what I do. I'll e'en to bed as soon as I have told you that I am very much

Your faithful friend
and servant,
D. Osborne

We know from her brother's diary that Dorothy's visit to London was accomplished. She and Temple met for the first time after a separation of at least eighteen months.

She stayed in lodgings with her aunt, Lady Gargrave. Two short notes have survived from this visit, both written on February 14th. In the first, she gives Temple her address and asks him to call on the following morning, Tuesday:

SIR, This is to tell you that you will be expected tomorrow morning about nine o'clock at a lodging over against the place where Charing Cross stood and the doors above the Goat Tavern. If with these directions you can find it out you will find there one that is very much

Your servant.

This note crossed with one from Temple in which he apparently complained of not having seen her on the Saturday or Sunday. Dorothy hastened to send a note of explanation:

You are mistaken if you think I am in debt for both these days. Saturday I confess was devoted to my Lady, but yesterday though I rose with good intentions of going to church, my cold would not suffer me but kept me prisoner all the day. I sent to your lodging to tell you that visiting the sick was part of the work of the day, but you were gone, and so I went to bed again where your letter found me this morning, but now I will rise and dispatch some visits that I owe that tomorrow may be entirely

Yours.

Letter 8

Dorothy wrote to Temple immediately on her return home to Chicksands. She is still suffering from the cold she had had before setting out for London.

(TUESDAY FEBRUARY THE 22ND, 1653)

SIR, Though I am very weary after my journey, and not well, having added much to a sufficient cold I had at London, yet guessing at your inclinations by my own, I thought you would be pleased to hear how we got home, and therefore resolved to say something, though it were nonsense, rather than omit the giving you a satisfaction that is in my power. I am so perfectly dosed with my cold and my journey together that all I can say is that I am here, and that I have only so much sense left as to wish you were so too. When that leaves me you may conclude me past all;—till then I'm sure I shall be

Your faithful friend and servant.

CHICKSANDS.

Letter 9

Dorothy tells Temple not to be so much upset by their separation. She approves of his plan to accompany Lord Lisle to Sweden, as she wishes him

to do everything that will ensure good relations with his father. She comments on her reading of French memoirs and romances.

[SATURDAY FEBRUARY THE 26TH, 1653]

SIR, I was so kind as to write to you by the coachman, and let me tell you I think 'twas the greatest testimony of my friendship that I could give you; for, trust me, I was so tired with my journey, so dosed with my cold, and so out of humour with our parting, that I should have done it with great unwillingness to anybody else. I lay abed all next day to recover myself, and rose a Thursday to receive your letter with the more ceremony. I found no fault with the ill writing, 'twas but too easy to read, methought, for I am sure I had done much sooner than I could have wished. But, in earnest, I was heartily troubled to find you in so much disorder. I would not have you so kind to me as to be cruel to yourself, in whom I am more concerned. No; for God sake, let us not make afflictions of such things as these; I am afraid we shall meet with too many real ones.

I am glad your journey holds, because I think 'twill be a good diversion for you this summer; but I admire your father's patience, that lets you rest with so much indifference when there is such a fortune offered. I'll swear I have great scruples of conscience myself in the point, and am much afraid I am not your friend if I am any part of the occasion that hinders you from accepting it. Yet I am sure my intentions towards you are very innocent and good, for you are one of those whose interests I shall ever prefer much above my own; and you are not to thank me for it, since, to speak truth, I secure my own by it; for I defy my ill fortune to make me miserable, unless she does it in the persons of my friends. I wonder how your father came to know I was in town, unless my old friend, your cousin Hammond,* should tell him. Pray, for my sake, be a very obedient son; all your faults will be laid to my charge else, and, alas! I have too many of my own.

You say nothing how your sister does,† which makes me hope

* Temple's cousin, Colonel Robert Hammond, who was Governor of the Isle of Wight when Dorothy and Temple met there in 1648.

† Temple's sister Martha, who was living in London at the time with him and his father, Sir John Temple. In 1662 she married Sir Thomas

35

there is no more of danger in her sickness. Pray, when it may be no trouble to her, tell her how much I am her servant; and have a care of yourself this cold weather. I have read your *Reine Marguerite*,* and will return it you when you please. If you will have my opinion of her, I think she had a good deal of wit, and a great deal of patience for a woman of so high a spirit. She speaks with too much indifference of her husband's several amours, and commends Bussy as if she were a little concerned in him. I think her a better sister than a wife, and believe she might have made a better wife to a better husband. But the story of Mademoiselle de Tournon is so sad, that when I had read it I was able to go no further, and was fain to take up something else to divert myself withal. Have you read *Cleopatra*? I have six tomes on't here that I can lend you if you have not; there are some stories in't you will like, I believe. But what an ass am I to think you can be idle enough at London to read romances! No, I'll keep them till you come hither;† here they may be welcome to you for want of better company. Yet, that you may not imagine we are quite out of the world here, and so be frighted from coming, I can assure you we are seldom without news, such as it is; and at this present we do abound with stories of my Lady Sunderland and Mr. Smith; with what reverence he approaches her, and how like a gracious princess she receives him, that they say 'tis worth one's going twenty miles to see it. All our ladies are mightily pleased with the example, but I do not find that the men intend to follow it, and I'll undertake Sir Solomon Justinian wishes her in the Indies, for fear she should pervert his new wife.

Your fellow-servant‡ kisses your hands, and says, 'If you mean to make love to her old woman this is the best time you can take, for she is dying; this cold weather kills her, I think.' It has

* *Mémoires de la Reyne Marguerite*, Paris, 1628. Margaret of Valois, the divorced wife of Henry of Navarre.
† As far as we know, this visit never materialized.
‡ Dorothy's companion and chaperone, Jane.

Giffard, who died two weeks later. She then lived with Dorothy and William. She left a manuscript life of her brother, whom she outlived. It was she who was left to squabble with Jonathan Swift over her brother's literary remains. Esther Johnson, Swift's unfortunate Stella, was her maid.

undone me, I am sure, in killing an old knight that I have been waiting for this seven year, and now he dies and will leave me nothing, I believe, but leaves a rich widow for somebody. I think you had best come awooing to her; I have a good interest in her, and it shall be all employed in your service if you think fit to make any addresses there. But to be sober now again, for God sake send me word how your journey goes forward, when you think you shall begin it, and how long it may last, when I may expect your coming this way; and of all things, remember to provide a safe address for your letters when you are abroad. This is a strange, confused one, I believe; for I have been called away twenty times, since I sat down to write it, to my father, who is not very well; but you will pardon it—we are past ceremony, and excuse me if I say no more now that I am *toujours la mesme*, that is, ever

Your affectionate
friend and servant.

Letter 10

Dorothy gives an amusing account of the arrival of Temple's last letter during a game of cards with Mrs Thorold, the granddaughter of her aunt, Lady Gargrave. Mrs Thorold had recently been widowed.

Dorothy discusses the match that has been proposed between Temple and a Mrs Cl.

[SATURDAY MARCH THE 5TH, 1653]

SIR, Your last letter came like a pardon to one upon the block. I have given over the hopes on't, having received my letters by the other carrier, who uses always to be last. The loss put me hugely out of order, and you would both have pitied and laughed at me if you could have seen how woodenly I entertained the widow, who came hither the day before, and surprised me very much. Not being able to say anything, I got her to cards, and there with a great deal of patience lost my money to her—or rather I gave it as my ransom. In the midst of our play, in comes my blessed boy with your letter, and, in earnest, I was not able to disguise the joy it gave me, though one was by that is not much your friend,* and took notice of a blush that for my life I could not keep back. I put up the letter in my pocket, and made what haste I could to lose the money I had left, that I might take occasion to go fetch some more; but I did not make such haste back again, I can assure you. I took time enough to have coined myself some money if I had had the art on't, and left my brother enough to make all his addresses to her if he were so disposed. I know not whether he was pleased or not, but I am sure I was.

You make so reasonable demands that 'tis not fit you should be denied. You ask my thoughts but at one hour; you will think me bountiful, I hope, when I shall tell you that I know no hour when you have them not. No, in earnest, my very dreams are yours, and I have got such a habit of thinking of you that any other thought intrudes and grows uneasy to me. I drink your health every morning in a drench that would poison a horse I believe, and 'tis the only way I have to persuade myself to take it. 'Tis the infusion of steel,† and makes me so horribly sick, that every day at ten o'clock I am making my will and taking leave of all my friends. You will believe you are not forgot then. They tell me I must take this ugly drink a fortnight, and then begin another as bad; but unless you say so too, I do not think I shall. 'Tis worse than dying by the half.

I am glad your father is so kind to you. I shall not dispute it with him, because 'tis much more in his power than in mine, but I shall never yield that 'tis more in his desires. Sure he was much pleased with that which was a truth when you told it him, but would have been none if he had asked the question sooner. He thought there was no danger of you since you were more ignorant and less concerned in my being in town than he. If I were Mrs. Cl., he would be more my friend; but, howsoever, I am much his servant as he is your father. I have sent you your book. And since you are at leisure to consider the moon, you may be enough to read *Cleopatra*, therefore I have sent you three tomes;

* Henry Osborne, Dorothy's brother. He took an unfavourable view of their association.

† Powdered steel in water, a fashionable remedy at the time.

when you have done with those you shall have the rest, and I believe they will please. There is a story of Artemise that I will recommend to you; her disposition I like extremely, it has a great deal of gratitude in't; and if you meet with one Brittomart, pray send me word how you like him. I am not displeased that my Lord [Lisle] makes no more haste, for though I am very willing you should go the journey for many reasons, yet two or three months hence, sure, will be soon enough to visit so cold a country, and I would not have you endure two winters in one year. Besides, I look for my eldest brother and my cousin Molle here shortly, and I should be glad to have nobody to entertain but you, whilst you are here. Lord! that you had the invisible ring, or Fortunatus his wishing hat;* now, at this instant, you should be here.

My brother is gone to wait upon the widow homewards—she that was born to persecute you and I, I think. She has so tired me with being here but two days, that I do not think I shall accept of the offer she made me of living with her in case my father dies before I have disposed of myself. Yet we are very great [friends,] and for my comfort she says she will come again about the latter end of June and stay longer with me. My aunt is still in town, kept by her business, which I am afraid will not go well, they do so delay it; and my precious uncle† does so visit her, and is so kind, that without doubt some mischief will follow. Do you know his son, my cousin Harry? 'Tis a handsome youth, and well-natured, but such a goose; and he has bred him so strangely, that he needs all his ten thousand pound a year. I would fain have him marry my Lady Diana, she was his mistress when he was a boy. He had more wit then than he has now, I think, and I have less wit than he, sure, for spending my paper upon him when I have so little. Here is hardly

room for your affectionate friend and servant.

* The ring by which Gyges, a Lydian shepherd, made himself invisible and seduced the wife of Candaules and made himself king (Plato's *Republic*). The story of Fortunatus was dramatized by Dekker in 1600. The Sultan gave Fortunatus a cap which he had only to put on and wish, to find himself transported to wherever he wanted.

† Sir John Danvers and his son Henry. The latter died in 1654. Dorothy hoped his fortune would attract her friend Lady Diana Rich.

Letter 11

Dorothy tells Temple that she has been taking an infusion of steel for 'the spleen', one of her periodic attacks of depression. She advises Temple in the business of the proposed marriage between him and a Mrs Cl. She says she is well fitted for the task, as she has just been interrogated by her brothers on the subject of her own marriage. She reveals her determination not to be hurried into a marriage of convenience to suit them.

[SATURDAY MARCH THE 12TH, 1653]

SIR, I am so far from thinking you ill-natured for wishing I might not outlive you, that I should not have thought you at all kind if you had done otherwise; no, in earnest, I was never yet so in love with my life but that I could have parted with it upon a much less occasion than your death, and 'twill be no compliment to you to say it would be very uneasy to me then, since 'tis not very pleasant to me now. Yet you will say I take great pains to preserve it, as ill as I like it; but no, I'll swear 'tis not that I intend in what I do; all that I aim at is but to keep myself from growing a beast. They do so fright me with strange stories of what the spleen will bring me to in time, that I am kept in awe with them like a child; they tell me 'twill not leave me common sense, that I shall hardly be fit company for my own dogs, and that it will end either in a stupidness that will make me incapable of anything, or fill my head with such whims as will make me ridiculous. To prevent this, who would not take steel or anything—though I am partly of your opinion that 'tis an ill kind of physic. Yet I am confident that I take it the safest way, for I do not take the powder, as many do, but only lay a piece of steel in white wine over night and drink the infusion next morning, which one would think were nothing, and yet 'tis not to be imagined how sick it makes me for an hour or two, and, which is the misery, all that time one must be using some kind of exercise. Your fellow-servant* has a blessed time on't. I make her play at shuttlecock with me, and she is the veriest bungler at it ever you saw. Then am I ready to beat her with the battledore, and grow so peevish

* Jane, Dorothy's companion.

40

as I grow sick, that I'll undertake she wishes there were no steel in England. But then to recompense the morning, I am in good humour all the day after for joy that I am well again. I am told 'twill do me good, and am content to believe; if it does not, I am but where I was.

I do not use to forget my old acquaintances. Almanzor* is as fresh in my memory as if I had visited his tomb but yesterday, though it be at least seven years agone since. You will believe I had not been used to great afflictions when I made his story such a one to me, as I cried an hour together for him, and was so angry with Alcidiana that for my life I could never love her after it. You do not tell me whether you received the books I sent you, but I will hope you did, because you say nothing to the contrary. They are my dear Lady Diana's, and therefore I am much concerned that they should be safe. And now I speak of her, she is acquainted with your aunt, my Lady R., and says all that you say of her. If her niece has so much wit, will you not be persuaded to like her; or say she has not quite so much, may not her fortune make it up? In earnest, I know not what to say, but if your father does not use all his kindness and all his power to make you consider your own advantage, he is not like other fathers. Can you imagine that he that demands £5,000 besides the reversion of an estate will like bare £4,000? Such miracles are seldom seen, and you must prepare to suffer a strange persecution unless you grow conformable; therefore consider what you do, 'tis the part of a friend to advise you. I could say a great deal to this purpose, and tell you that 'tis not discreet to refuse a good offer, nor safe to trust wholly to your own judgment in your disposal. I was never better provided in my life for a grave admonishing discourse. Would you had heard how I have been catechized for you, and seen how soberly I sit and answer to interrogatories. Would you think that upon examination it is found that you are not an indifferent person to me? But the mischief is, that what my intentions or resolutions are, is not to be discovered, though much pains has been taken to collect all scattering circumstances; and all the probable conjectures that can be raised from thence has been urged, to see if anything would be confessed. And all

* The hero of a Spanish romance, probably *Palmerin de Oliva*.

41

this done with so much ceremony and compliment, so many pardons asked for undertaking to counsel or inquire, and so great kindness and passion for all my interests professed, that I cannot but take it well, though I am very weary on't. You are spoken of with the reverence due to a person that I seem to like, and for as much as they know of you, you do deserve a very good esteem; but your fortune and mine can never agree, and, in plain terms, we forfeit our discretions and run wilfully upon our own ruins if there be such a thought. To all this I make no reply, but that if they will needs have it that I am not without kindness for you, they must conclude withal that 'tis no part of my intention to ruin you, and so the conference breaks up for that time. All this is [from] my friend, that is not yours; and the gentleman that came upstairs in a basket,* I could tell him that he spends his breath to very little purpose, and has but his labours for his pains. Without his precepts my own judgment would preserve me from doing any [thing] that might be prejudicial to you or unjustifiable to the world; but if these may be secured, nothing can alter the resolution I have taken of settling my whole stock of happiness upon the affection of a person that is dear to me, whose kindness I shall infinitely prefer before any other considera-tion whatsoever, and I shall not blush to tell you that you have made the whole world besides so indifferent to me that, if I cannot be yours, they may dispose me how they please. Henry Cromwell will be as acceptable to me as any one else.† If I may undertake to counsel, I think you shall do well to comply with your father as far as is possible, and not to discover‡ any aversion to what he desires farther than you can give reason for. What his

* Henry and John Osborne, her brothers. John was suffering from an ague at the time, which meant that he had to be carried upstairs. See Letter 13.
† Oliver Cromwell's second son. He seems to have been quite a different person from his father: Mrs Hutchinson described him as 'a debauched ungodly Cavalier', a judgement not to be taken too literally. He was undoubtedly no Puritan, but a man of the world, courteous and cheerful. Dorothy probably made his acquaintance for the first time during the short period when she was living in London just before going to St Malo to join her father in 1648.
‡ Reveal.

disposition may be I know not; but 'tis that of many parents to judge their children's dislikes to be an humour of approving nothing that is chosen for them, which many times makes them take up another of denying their children all they choose for themselves. I find I am in the humour of talking wisely if my paper would give me leave. 'Tis great pity here is room for no more but your faithful friend and servant.

Letter 12

A short note taken to Temple by Dorothy's companion, Jane, on her way to Guernsey.

[THURSDAY MARCH THE 17TH, 1653]

SIR, Your fellow-servant, upon the news you sent her, is going to look out her captain. In earnest now she is going to sea, but 'tis to Guernsey to her friends there. Her going is so sudden that I have not time to say much to you but that I long to hear what you have done, and that I shall hate myself as long as I live if I cause any disorder* between your father and you. But if my name can do you any service I shall not scruple to trust you with that, since I make none to trust you with my heart. She will direct you how you may send to me, and for God sake, though this be a short letter, let not yours be so. 'Tis very late and I am able to hold open my eyes no longer. Good-night! If I were not sure to meet you again by-and-bye I would not leave you so soon.

Your.

Letter 13

Dorothy has more to say on the subject of Temple and Mrs Cl. She has sent him further volumes of La Cléopâtre, and says she will write the following week with instructions for their delivery to Lady Diana Rich.

* Bad feeling, unpleasantness.

43

[SATURDAY MARCH THE 19TH, 1653]

SIR, I am glad you 'scaped a beating, but, in earnest, would it had lighted upon my brother's groom. I think I should have beaten him myself if I had been able. I have expected your letter all this day with the greatest impatience that was possible, and at last resolved to go out and meet the fellow; and when I came down to the stables, I found him come, had set up his horse, and was sweeping the stable in great order. I could not imagine him so very a beast as to think his horses were to be served before me, and therefore was presently struck with an apprehension he had no letter for me: it went cold to my heart as ice, and hardly left me courage enough to ask him the question; but when he had drawled it out that he thought there was a letter for me in his bag, I quickly made him leave his broom. 'Twas well 'tis a dull fellow, he could not but have discern'd else that I was strangely overjoyed with it, and earnest to have it; for though the poor fellow made what haste he could to untie his bag, I did nothing but chide him for being so slow. At last I had it, and, in earnest, I know not whether an entire diamond of the bigness on't would have pleased me half so well; if it would, it must be only out of this consideration, that such a jewel would make me rich enough to dispute you with Mrs. Cl., and perhaps make your father like me as well. I like him, I'll swear, and extremely too, for being so calm in a business where his desires were so much crossed. Either he has a great power over himself, or you have a great interest in him, or both. If you are pleased it should end thus, I cannot dislike it; but if it would have been happy for you, I should think myself strangely unfortunate in being the cause that it went no further. I cannot say that I prefer your interest before my own, because all yours are so much mine that 'tis impossible for me to be happy if you are not so; but if they could be divided I am certain I should. And though you reproached me with unkindness for advising you not to refuse a good offer, yet I shall not be discouraged from doing it again when there is occasion, for I am

44

resolved to be your friend whether you will or no. And, for example, though I know you do not need my counsel, yet I cannot but tell you that I think 'twere very well that you took some care to make my Lady R. your friend, and oblige her by your civilities to believe that you were sensible of the favour was offered you, though you had not the grace to make good use on't. In very good earnest now, she is a woman (by all that I have heard of her) that one would not lose; besides that, 'twill become you to make some satisfaction for downright refusing a young lady—'twas unmercifully done.

Would to God you would leave that trick of making excuses! Can you think it necessary to me, or believe that your letters can be so long as to make them unpleasing to me? Are mine so to you? If they are not, yours never will be so to me. You see I say anything to you, out of a belief that, though my letters were more impertinent than they are, you would not be without them nor wish them shorter. Why should you be less kind? If your fellow-servant has been with you, she has told you I part with her but for her advantage. That I shall always be willing to do; but whensoever she shall think fit to serve again, and is not provided of a better mistress, she knows where to find me.

I have sent you the rest of *Cleopatra*,* pray keep them all in your hands, and the next week I will send you a letter and directions where you shall deliver that and the books for my lady. Is it possible that she can be indifferent to anybody? Take heed of telling me such stories; if all those excellences she is rich in cannot keep warm a passion without the sunshine of her eyes, what are poor people to expect; and were it not a strange vanity in me to believe yours can be long-lived? It would be very pardonable in you to change, but, sure, in him 'tis a mark of so great inconstancy as shows him of an humour that nothing can fix. When you go into the Exchange, pray call at the great shop above, 'The Flower Pott.' I spoke to Heams, the man of the shop, when I was in town, for a quart of orange-flower water; he had

---

* The sending of the previous parts is mentioned in Letters 9 and 10. Dorothy anglicizes the title of *La Cléopâtre* by La Valprenède, although she undoubtedly read it in the original French, published in Paris in ten volumes in 1647.

none that was good then, but promised to get me some. Pray put him in mind of it, and let him show it you before he sends it me, for I will not altogether trust to his honesty; you see I make no scruple of giving you little idle commissions, 'tis a freedom you allow me, and that I should be glad you would take. The Frenchman that set my seals lives between Salisbury House and the Exchange, at a house that was not finished when I was there, and the master of the shop, his name is Walker, he made me pay 50s. for three, but 'twas too dear. You will meet with a story in these parts of *Cleopatra* that pleased me more than any that ever I read in my life; 'tis of one Délie, pray give me your opinion of her and her prince. This letter is writ in great haste, as you may see; 'tis my brother's sick day, and I'm not willing to leave him long alone. I forgot to tell you in my last that he was come hither to try if he can lose an ague here that he got in Gloucestershire. He asked me for you very kindly, and if he knew I writ to you I should have something to say from him besides what I should say for myself if I had room.

Yrs.

Letter 14

Dorothy chides Temple with having taken her remarks about Lady Diana Rich's inconstant admirer in the wrong spirit. She discusses his proposed journey to Sweden, and indulges in some frank comment on the affairs of others.

[FRIDAY] MARCH THE 25TH [1653]

SIR, I know not how to oblige so civil a person as you are more than by giving you the occasion of serving a fair lady. In sober earnest, I know you will not think it a trouble to let your boy deliver those books and this enclosed letter where it is directed for my lady, whom I would, the fainest in the world, have you acquainted with, that you might judge whether I had not reason to say somebody was to blame. But had you reason to be displeased that I said a change in you would be much more pardonable than in him? Certainly you had not. I spake it very innocently,

46

and out of a great sense how much she deserves more than anybody else. I shall take heed though hereafter what I write, since you are so good at raising doubts to persecute yourself withal, and shall condemn my own easy faith no more; for sure 'tis a better-natured and a less fault to believe too much than to distrust where there is no cause. If you were not so apt to quarrel, I would tell you that I am glad to hear your journey goes forward,* but you would presently imagine that 'tis because I would be glad if you were gone; need I say that 'tis because I prefer your interests much before my own, because I would not have you lose so good a diversion and so pleasing an entertainment (as in all likelihood this voyage will be to you), and because, which is a powerful argument with me, the sooner you go, the sooner I may hope for your return. If it be necessary, I will confess all this, and something more, which is, that notwithstanding all my gallantry and resolution, 'tis much for my credit that my courage is put to no greater a trial than parting with you at this distance. But you are not going yet neither, and therefore we'll leave the discourse on't till then, if you please, for I find no great entertainment in't. And let me ask you whether it be possible that Mr. Grey† makes love, they say he does, to my Lady Jane Seymour? If it were expected that one should give a reason for their passions, what could he say for himself? He would not offer, sure, to make us believe my Lady Jane a lovelier person than my Lady Anne Percy. I did not think I should have lived to have seen his frozen heart melted, 'tis the greatest conquest she will ever make; may it be happy to her, but in my opinion he has not a good-natured look. The younger brother was a servant, a great while, to my fair neighbour,‡ but could not be received; and in earnest I could not blame her. I was his confidante and heard him make his

* Temple's journey to Sweden with Lord Lisle was still being contemplated (see Letters 6 and 9).

† It has so far been impossible to identify this gentleman, of whom Dorothy had such a poor opinion. Whoever he was, neither of the ladies mentioned married him. Lady Jane Seymour, youngest daughter of the Duke of Somerset, married Viscount Dungarvan, and Lady Anne Percy, daughter of the Earl of Northumberland, married Philip Stanhope, later Lord Chesterfield.

‡ Lady Grey de Ruthin, a peeress in her own right, and still unmarried.

addresses; not that I brag of the favour he did me, for anybody might have been so that had been as often there, and he was less scrupulous in that point than one would have been that had had less reason. But in my life I never heard a man say more, nor less to the purpose; and if his brother have not a better gift in court-ship, he will owe my lady's favour to his fortune rather than to his address. My Lady Anne Wentworth* I hear is marrying, but I cannot learn to whom; nor is it easy to guess who is worthy of her. In my judgment she is, without dispute, the finest lady I know (one always excepted);† not that she is at all handsome, but infinitely virtuous and discreet, of a sober and very different humour from most of the young people of these times, but has as much wit and is as good company as anybody that ever I saw. What would you give that I had but the wit to know when to make an end of my letters? Never anybody was persecuted with such long epistles; but you will pardon my unwillingness to leave you, and notwithstanding all your little doubts, believe that I am very much

Your faithful friend
and humble servant,
D. Osborne.

Letter 15

Dorothy is very sensible of the danger to her health of her fits of depression, although she makes light of Jane's account of them to Temple. She asks him to be equally conscious of his own health. Once again, she speaks of Temple's father and his doubts and fears for his son's future. She mentions her own good fortune in having a father who has not pressed her to marry, and assures Temple of her determination to prefer no other man.

[TUESDAY MARCH THE 29TH, 1653]

SIR, There shall be two posts this week, for my brother sends his groom up, and I am resolved to make some advantage of it.

* Daughter of Lord Strafford, who had been executed in 1641. She married Lord Rockingham. She is mentioned again in Letter 34.
† This is probably a reference to Lady Diana Rich.

Pray, what the paper denied me in your last, let me receive by him. Your fellow-servant is a sweet jewel to tell tales of me. The truth is, I cannot deny but that I have been very careless of myself, but, alas! who would have been other? I never thought my life a thing worth my care whilst nobody was concerned in't but myself; now I shall look upon't as something that you would not lose, and therefore shall endeavour to keep it for you. But then you must return my kindness with the same care of a life that's much dearer to me. I shall not be so unreasonable as to desire that, for my satisfaction, you should deny yourself a recreation that is pleasing to you, and very innocent, sure, when 'tis not used in excess, but I cannot consent you should disorder yourself with it, and Jane was certainly in the right when she told you I would have chid if I had seen you so endanger a health that I am so much concerned in. But for what she tells you of my melancholy you must not believe; she thinks nobody in good humour unless they laugh perpetually, as Nan* and she does, which I was never given to much, and now I have been so long accustomed to my own natural dull humour nothing can alter it. 'Tis not that I am sad (for as long as you and the rest of my friends are well), I thank God I have no occasion to be so, but I never appear to be very merry, and if I had all that I could wish for in the world, I do not think it would make any visible change in my humour. And yet with all my gravity I could not but laugh at your encounter in the Park, though I was not pleased that you should leave a fair lady and go lie upon the cold ground. That is full as bad as over-heating yourself at tennis,† and therefore remember 'tis one of the things you are forbidden. You have reason to think your father kind, and I have reason to think him very civil; all his scruples are very just ones, but such as times and a little good fortune (if we were either of us lucky to it) might satisfy. He may be confident I can never think of disposing myself

* Nan Stacy, a young woman of Jane's age. She may at some time have been a servant of Dorothy's, but later seems to have been living in London. Temple may well have lodged with her and her mother.
† Temple was very fond of the game, and there are many references elsewhere to it as his favourite sport. He continued to play long after he and Dorothy were married. It is interesting to notice that despite Puritan disapproval the game was still being played in London.

without my father's consent; and though he has left it more in my power than almost anybody leaves a daughter, yet certainly I were the worst natured person in the world if his kindness were not a greater tie upon me than any advantage he could have reserved. Besides that, 'tis my duty, from which nothing can ever tempt me, nor could you like it in me if I should do otherwise, 'twould make me unworthy of your esteem; but if ever that may be obtained, or I left free, and you in the same condition, all the advantages of fortune or person imaginable met together in one man should not be preferred before you. I think I cannot leave you better than with this assurance. 'Tis very late, and having been abroad all this day, I knew not till e'en now of this messenger. Good-night to you. There needed no excuse for the conclusion of your letter. Nothing can please me better. Once more good-night. I am half in a dream already.

Your.

FOR MR. TEMPLE.

Letter 16

This is one of the last letters in which Dorothy signs herself as 'servant'. In his answer to Letter 22 Temple objects to her use of the word, and it only recurs in Letter 50, when Dorothy reverts to a more formal style at a time when it seemed that their more intimate relationship must come to an end.

[SATURDAY APRIL THE 2ND, 1653]

SIR, I did receive both your letters, and yet was not satisfied but resolved to have a third. You had defeated me strangely if it had been a blank. Not that I should have taken it ill, for 'tis as impossible for me to do so as for you to give me the occasion. But though by sending a blank with your name to it you had given me a power to please myself, yet I should ne'er have done it half so well as your letter did, for nothing pleases me like being assured that you are pleased. Will you forgive me if I make this a short letter? In earnest I have so many to write and so little time to do it that for this once I think I could employ a secretary if

I had one. Yet here's another letter for you, though I know not whether it is such a one as you desire, but if it be not you must thank yourself. If you had given larger instructions, you had been better obeyed, and notwithstanding all my haste, I cannot but tell you, 'twas a little unkind to ask me if I could do it for your satisfaction. So poor a thing as that? If I had time I would chide you for it extremely and make you know that there is nothing I cannot do for the satisfaction of a person I esteem and to whom I shall always be

a faithful friend and servant.

Letter 17

Dorothy writes of her father's illness. We know from Henry Osborne's diary that Sir Peter had been taken ill in church on April 10th. Nursing her father was to occupy much of Dorothy's time during the coming year and to aggravate her natural tendency to fits of melancholy.

[THURSDAY APRIL THE 14TH, 1653]

SIR, I received your letter to-day, when I thought it almost impossible that I should be sensible of anything but my father's sickness and my own affliction in it. Indeed, he was then so dangerously ill that we could not reasonably hope he should outlive this day; yet he is now, I thank God, much better, and I am come so much to myself with it, as to undertake a long letter to you whilst I watch by him. Towards the latter end it will be excellent stuff, I believe; but, alas! you may allow me to dream sometimes. I have had so little sleep since my father was sick that I am never thoroughly awake. Lord, how have I wished for you! Here do I sit all night by a poor moped fellow that serves my father, and have much ado to keep him awake and myself too. If you heard the wise discourse that is between us, you would swear we wanted sleep; but I shall leave him to night to entertain himself, and try if I can write as wisely as I talk. I am glad all is well again. In earnest, it would have lain upon my conscience if I had been the occasion of making your poor boy lose a service, that if he has the wit to know how to value it, he would never have forgiven it me while he had lived.

But while I remember it, let me ask you if you did not send my letter and *Cleopatra* where I directed you for my lady. I received one from her to-day full of the kindest reproaches, that she has not heard from me this three weeks. I have writ constantly to her, but I do not so much wonder that the rest are lost, as that she seems not to have received that which I sent to you nor the books. I do not understand it, but I know there is no fault of yours in't. But, hark you! if you think to 'scape with sending me such bits of letters, you are mistaken. You say you are often interrupted, and I believe it; but you must use then to begin to write before you receive mine, and whensoever you have any spare time allow me some of it. Can you doubt that anything can make your letters cheap? In earnest, 'twas unkindly said, and if I could be angry with you it should be for that. No, certainly they are, and ever will be, dear to me as that which I receive a huge contentment by. How shall I long when you are gone your journey to hear from you! how shall I apprehend a thousand accidents that are not likely nor will never happen, I hope! Oh, if you do not send me long letters, then you are the cruellest person that can be! If you love me you will; and if you do not, I shall never love myself. You need not fear such a command as you mention. Alas! I am too much concerned that you should love me ever to forbid it you; 'tis all that I propose of happiness to myself in the world. The turning of my paper has waked me;* all this while I was in a dream. But 'tis no matter, I am content you should know they are of you, and that when my thoughts are left most at liberty they are the kindest. I'll swear my eyes are so heavy that I hardly see what or how I write, nor do I think you will be able to read it when I have done; the best on't is 'twill be no great loss to you if you do not, for, sure, the greatest part on't is not sense, and yet on my conscience I shall go on with it. 'Tis like people that talk in their sleep, nothing interrupts them but talking to them again, and that you are not like to do at this distance; besides that, at this instant you are, I believe, more asleep than I, and do not so much as dream that I am writing

* Dorothy turned the paper in order to write in the margin.

to you. My fellow-watchers have been asleep too, till just now they begin to stretch and yawn; they are going to try if eating and drinking can keep them awake, and I am kindly invited to be of their company; my father's man has got one of the maids to talk nonsense to to-night, and they have got between them a bottle of ale. I shall lose my share if I do not take them at their first offer. Your patience till I have drunk, and then I am for you again.

And now in the strength of this ale, I believe I shall be able to fill up this paper that's left with something or other; and first let me ask you if you have seen a book of poems newly come out, made by my Lady Newcastle?* For God's sake if you meet with it send it me; they say 'tis ten times more extravagant than her dress. Sure, the poor woman is a little distracted, she could never be so ridiculous else as to venture at writing books, and in verse too. If I should not sleep this fortnight I should not come to that. My eyes grow a little dim though, for all the ale, and I believe if I could see it this is most strangely scribbled. Sure, I shall not find fault with your writing in haste, for anything but the shortness of your letter; and 'twould be very unjust in me to tie you to a ceremony that I do not observe myself. No, for God sake let there be no such thing between us; a real kindness is so far beyond all compliment, that it never appears more than when there is least of t'other mingled with it. If, then, you would have me believe yours to be perfect, confirm it to me by a kind freedom. Tell me if there be anything that I can serve you in, employ me as you would do that sister that you say you love so well. Chide me when I do anything that is not well, but then make haste to tell me that you have forgiven me, and that you are what I shall ever be,

a faithful friend.

* Margaret, wife of William Cavendish, Marquis (later Duke) of Newcastle, published a collection called *Poems and Fancies*, and later a supplementary volume called *Philosophical Fancies*, which Dorothy makes a passing reference to in Letter 57.

Letter 18

Dorothy talks about an event that took place on April 20th, 1653: Cromwell's dissolution of Parliament. The news of this would only have taken a day or two to reach Chicksands, and she is bursting to have some of the rumours associated with it confirmed. She rightly supposes that the coup d'état will delay Temple's proposed journey to Sweden.

[SATURDAY APRIL THE 23RD, 1653]

SIR, That you may be sure it was a dream that I writ that part of my letter in, I do not now remember what it was I writ, but seems it was very kind, and possibly you owe the discovery on't to my being asleep. But I do not repent it, for I should not love you if I did not think you discreet enough to be trusted with the knowledge of all my kindness. Therefore 'tis not that I desire to hide it from you, but that I do not love to tell it; and perhaps if you could read my heart, I should make less scruple of your seeing on't there than in my letters.

I can easily guess who the pretty young lady is, for there are but two in England of that fortune, and they are sisters, but I am to seek who the gallant should be. If it be no secret, you may tell me. However, I shall wish him all good success if he be your friend, as I suppose he is by his confidence in you. If it be neither of the Spencers, I wish it were; I have not seen two young men that looked as if they deserved good fortunes so much as those brothers.

But bless me, what will become of us all now? Is not this a strange turn?* What does my Lord Lisle? Sure this will at least defer your journey? Tell me what I must think on't; whether it be better or worse, or whether you are at all concern'd in't? For if you are not I am not, only if I had been so wise as to have taken hold of the offer was made me by Henry Cromwell,† I might have been in a fair way of preferment, for, sure, they will be greater now than ever. Is it true that Algernon Sydney‡ was so unwilling

---

* Cromwell's *coup d'état*.　　　† See Letter 11.

‡ See Letter 7. One of the best accounts of what happened in Parliament on April 20th is to be found in the diary of Sydney's father, Lord

to leave the House, that the General was fain to take the pains to turn him out himself? Well, 'tis a pleasant world this. If Mr. Pym★ were alive again, I wonder what he would think of these proceedings, and whether this would appear as great a breach of the Privilege of Parliament as the demanding the 5 members?† But I shall talk treason by and by if I do not look to myself. 'Tis safer talking of the orange-flower water you sent me. The carrier has given me a great charge to tell you that it came safe, and I must do him right. As you say, 'tis not the best I have seen, nor the worst.

I shall expect your Diary next week, though this will be but a short letter: you may allow me to make excuses too sometimes; but, seriously, my father is now so continually ill, that I have hardly time for anything. 'Tis but an ague that he has, but yet I am much afraid that is more than his age and weakness will be able to bear; he keeps his bed, and never rises but to have it made, and most times faints with that. You ought in charity to write as much as you can, for, in earnest, my life here since my father's sickness is so sad that, to another humour than mine, it would be unsupportable; but I have been so used to misfortunes, that I cannot be much surprised with them, though perhaps I am as sensible of them as another. I'll leave you, for I find these thoughts begin to put me in ill humour; farewell, may you be ever happy. If I am so at all, it is in being

Your.

Letter 19

Dorothy is ill and has had two fits of 'ague'. She comments on Temple's diary which she had been looking forward to reading. She says nothing will

★ John Pym, the most powerful member of the Long Parliament.
† On January 2nd, 1642, John Pym was impeached with four other members, and two days later the King came to the House to arrest them. They had already taken refuge in the City and on the 11th they were escorted in triumph back to the House.

Leicester, in the *Sydney Papers*. Two of Cromwell's officers were ordered to throw Sydney out of the House, but he left of his own accord.

*persuade her to accept his offer to release her from the understanding or
unofficial engagement that exists between them. She asks him about his plans
for the immediate future.*

SIR, I am sorry my last letter frighted you so; 'twas no part of
my intention it should; but I am more sorry to see by your first
chapter* that your humour is not always so good as I could wish
it. 'Twas the only thing I ever desired we might differ in, and
therefore I think it is denied me. Whilst I read the description
on't, I could not believe but that I had writ it myself, it was so
much my own. I pity you in earnest much more than I do myself;
and yet I may deserve yours when I shall have told you, that
besides all that you speak of, I have gotten an ague that with two
fits has made me so very weak, that I doubted extremely yesterday
whether I should be able to sit up to-day to write to you. But
you must not be troubled at this; that's the way to kill me indeed. Besides, it is impossible I should keep it long, for here is my
eldest brother, and my cousin Molle, and two or three more of
them that have great understanding in agues, as people that have
been long acquainted with them, and they do so tutor and govern
me, that I am neither to eat, drink, nor sleep without their leave;
and, sure, my obedience deserves they should cure me, or else
they are great tyrants to very little purpose. You cannot imagine
how cruel they are to me, and yet will persuade me 'tis for my
good. I know they mean it so, and therefore say nothing but
submit, and sigh to think those are not here that would be kinder
to me. But you were cruel yourself when you seemed to apprehend I might oblige you to make good your last offer.† Alas! if I
could purchase the empire of the world at that rate, I should
think it much too dear; and though, perhaps, I am too unhappy
myself ever to make anybody else happy, yet, sure, I shall take
heed that my misfortunes may not prove infectious to my friends.
You ask counsel of a person that is very little able to give it. I

* Presumably Temple's diary which she was expecting in Letter 18 has
arrived and she has been reading the first entries.
† Temple had been disturbed by Letter 18, and may well have offered
to release Dorothy from their quasi-engagement.

cannot imagine whither you should go, since this journey is broke.* You must e'en be content to stay at home, I think, and see what will become of us, though I expect nothing of good; and, sure, you never made a truer remark in your life than that all changes are for the worse. Will it not stay your father's journey too?† Methinks it should. For God sake write me all that you hear or can think of, that I may have something to entertain myself withal. I have a scurvy head that will not let me write longer.

I am your.

FOR MRS. PAINTER, AT HER HOUSE
IN BEDFORD STREET, NEXT Yᵉ GOATE,
IN COVENT GARDEN.

Letter 20

Dorothy is recovering from her ague. She is pleased that Temple has at last met her friend Lady Diana Rich. She gives him a playful account of a new suitor.

[SATURDAY MAY THE 7TH, 1653]

SIR, I do not know that anybody has frighted me, or beaten me, or put me into more passion than what I usually carry about me, but yesterday I missed my fit, and am not without hope I shall hear no more on't. My father has lost his too, and my eldest brother, but we all look like people risen from the dead. Only my cousin Molle keeps his still; and, in earnest, I am not certain whether he would lose it or not, for it gives him a lawful occasion of being nice and cautious about himself, to which he in his own

---

* Lord Lisle had resigned his embassy to Sweden as a result of Cromwell's *coup d'état*, thus making Temple temporarily unemployed.
† The possibility of Sir John Temple being sent to Ireland had obviously already been discussed. In November, five months later, he was appointed as a commissioner to Ireland to advise on the rights of the Irish to estates in Ireland after the rebellion.

humour is so much inclined that 'twere not easy for him to forbear it. You need not send me my Lady Newcastle's book* at all, for I have seen it, and am satisfied that there are many soberer people in Bedlam. I'll swear her friends are much to blame to let her go abroad.

But I am hugely pleased that you have seen my Lady. I knew you could not choose but like her; but yet, let me tell you, you have seen but the worst of her. Her conversation has more charms than can be in mere beauty, and her humour and disposition would make a deformed person appear lovely. You had strange luck to meet my brother so soon. He went up but last Tuesday. I heard from him on Thursday, but he did not tell me he had seen you; perhaps he did not think it convenient to put me in mind of you; besides, he thought he told me enough in telling me my cousin Osborne was married.† Why did not you send me that news and a garland? Well, the best on't is I have a squire now that is as good as a knight.‡ He was coming as fast as a coach and six horses could bring him, but I desired him to stay till my ague was gone, and give me a little time to recover my good looks; for I protest if he saw me now he would never desire to see me again. Oh, me! I can but think how I shall sit like the lady of the lobster,§ and give audience at Babram.|| You have been there, I am sure. Nobody that is at Cambridge 'scapes it. But you were never so welcome thither as you shall be when I am mistress on't. In the meantime, I have sent you the first tome of *Cyrus* to read;¶ when you have done with it, leave it at Mr. Hollingsworth's, and I'll send you another. I have had ladies with me all this afternoon that are for London to-morrow, and now

---

* See Letter 17.

† Sir Thomas Osborne, an earlier suitor of Dorothy's (see Letter 3).

‡ The new suitor, referred to in Letter 21 as Mr B, has been identified as Levinus Bennet, Sheriff of Cambridgeshire.

§ A popular expression for the calcareous structure in the stomach of a lobster, supposed to resemble a seated female figure.

|| Or Babraham, where Levinus Bennet lived, six miles south-west of Cambridge.

¶ Temple had obviously finished *La Cléopâtre* and Dorothy now sends him *Artamène, ou le Grand Cyrus*, by Georges de Scudéry and his sister Madeleine, and published between 1649 and 1653.

have I as many letters to write as my Lord General's Secretary. Forgive me that this is no longer, for I am

Your.

Letter 21

Temple had already heard about the Sheriff of Cambridgeshire, and Dorothy complains playfully that there is no point in her writing of new suitors if he knows about them beforehand. She tells him why she cannot contemplate a trip to town in the near future, her father's illness being the main reason, although she herself is greatly recovered.

[SATURDAY MAY THE 14TH, 1653]

SIR, I tell you no more of my servants. I can no sooner give you some little hints whereabouts they live, but you know them presently,* and I meant you should be beholding to me for your acquaintance. But it seems this gentleman is not of so easy access, but that you may acknowledge something due to me, if I incline him to look graciously upon you, and therefore there is not much harm done. What has kept him from marrying all this while, or how the humour comes so furiously upon him now, I know not; but if he may be believed, he is resolved to be a most romance squire, and go in quest of some enchanted damsel, whom if he likes, as to her person (for fortune is a thing below him)—and we do not read in history that any knight or squire was ever so discourteous as to inquire what portions their ladies had—then he comes with the power of the county to demand her (which for the present he may dispose of, being Sheriff), so I do not see who is able to resist him. All that is to be hoped is, that since he may reduce whomsoever he pleases to his obedience, he will be very curious in his choice, and then I am secure.

It may be I dreamt it that you had met my brother, or else it was one of the reveries of my ague; if so, I hope I shall fall into

* Immediately, instantly.

no more of them. I have missed four fits, and had but five, and have recovered so much strength as made me venture to meet your letter on Wednesday, a mile from home. Yet my recovery will be nothing towards my leaving this place, where many reasons will oblige me to stay at least all this summer, unless some great alteration should happen in this family; that which I most own is my father's ill-health, which, though it be not in that extremity it has been, yet keeps him still a prisoner to his chamber, and for the most part to his bed, which is reason enough. But, besides, I can give you others. I am here much more out of people's way than in town, where my aunt and such as pretend an interest in me, and a power over me, do so persecute me with their good motions, and take it so ill that they are not accepted, as I would live in a hollow tree to avoid them. Here I have nobody but my brother to torment me, whom I can take the liberty to dispute with, and whom I have prevailed with hitherto to bring none of his pretenders to this place, because of the noise all such people make in a country, and the tittle-tattle it breeds amongst neighbours that have nothing to do but to inquire who marries and who makes love. If I can but keep him still in that humour, Mr. Bennet and I are likely to preserve our state and treat at distance like princes; but we have not sent one another our pictures yet, though my cousin Molle, who was his agent here, begged mine very earnestly. But, I thank God, an imagination took him one morning that he was falling into a dropsy, and make him in such haste to go back to Cambridge to his doctor, that he never remembered anything he had to ask of me, but the coach to carry him away. I lent it most willingly, and gone he is. My eldest brother goes up to town on Monday too; perhaps you may see him, but I cannot direct you where to find him, for he is not yet resolved himself where to lie; only 'tis likely Nan may tell you when he is there. He will make no stay, I believe. You will think him altered (and, if it be possible) more melancholy than he was. If marriage agrees no better with other people than it does with him, I shall pray that all my friends may 'scape it. Yet if I were my cousin, H. Danvers,* my Lady Diana

* Dorothy is repeating an earlier wish that her cousin should make a match with Lady Diana Rich. See Letter 10.

should not, if I could help it, as well as I love her: I would try if ten thousand pound a year with a husband that doted on her, as I should do, could not keep her from being unhappy. Well, in earnest, if I were a prince, that lady should be my mistress, but I can give no rule to anybody else, and perhaps those that are in no danger of losing their hearts to her may be infinitely taken with one I should not value at all; for (so say the Justinians)* wise Providence has ordained it that by their different humours everybody might find something to please themselves withal, without envying their neighbours. And now I have begun to talk gravely and wisely, I'll try if I can go a little further without being out.† No, I cannot, for I have forgot already what 'twas I would have said; but 'tis no matter, for, as I remember, it was not much to the purpose, and, besides, I have paper little enough left to chide you for asking so unkind a question as whether you were still the same in my thoughts. Have you deserved to be otherwise; that is, am I no more in yours? For till that be, 'tis impossible the other should; but that will never be, and I shall always be the same I am. My heart tells me so, and I may believe it; for if 'twere otherwise, Fortune would not persecute us thus. Oh, me! she's cruel, and how far her power may reach I know not, only I am sure, she cannot call back time that is past, and it is long since we resolved to be for ever most faithful friends.

Letter 22

Temple has said that they can hardly look forward to any great change in the present state of their relationship, and she agrees with him. She speaks of her brother at greater length than usual, giving a strong impression of the possessive nature of his feeling for her.

[SUNDAY MAY THE 22ND, 1653]

SIR, You must pardon me, I could not burn your other letter for my life; I was so pleased to see I had so much to read, and so sorry I had done so soon, that I resolved to begin them again, and had

* People like Sir Justinian Isham. See Letter 3.   † Losing myself.

like to have lost my dinner by it. I know not what humour you were in when you writ it; but Mr. Arbry's prophecy* and the falling down of the form did a little discompose my gravity. But I quickly recovered myself with thinking that you deserved to be chid for going where you knew you must of necessity lose your time. In earnest, I had a little scruple when I went with you thither,† and but that I was assured it was too late to go any whither else, and believed it better to hear an ill sermon than none, I think I should have missed his *belles remarques*. You had repented you, I hope, of that and all other your faults before you thought of dying.

What a satisfaction you had found out to make me for the injuries you say you have done me! And yet I cannot tell neither (though 'tis not the remedy I should choose) whether that were not a certain one for all my misfortunes; for, sure, I should have nothing then to persuade me to stay longer where they grow, and I should quickly take a resolution of leaving them and the world at once. I agree with you, too, that I do not see any great likelihood of the change of our fortunes, and that we have much more to wish than to hope for; but 'tis so common a calamity that I dare not murmur at it; better people have endured it, and I can give no reason why (almost) all are denied the satisfaction of disposing themselves to their own desires, but that it is a happiness too great for this world, and might endanger one's forgetting the next; whereas if we are crossed in that which only can make the world pleasing to us, we are quickly tired with the length of our journey and the disquiet of our inns, and long to be at home. One would think it were I that had heard the three sermons and were trying to make a fourth; these are truths that might become a pulpit better than Mr. Arbry's predictions. But lest you should think I have as many worms in my head as he, I'll give over in time, and tell you how far Mr. Luke‡ and I are acquainted. He

* The Rev. William Erbury, Anabaptist preacher and writer. He had a reputation for making wild predictions.

† Temple may have taken Dorothy to hear him preach when she was in London in February 1653.

‡ Probably one of the three sons of Sir Samuel Luke; Sir Samuel was an ardent Presbyterian and had been active in Cromwell's support. He was

lives within four or five miles of me, and one day that I had been to visit a lady that is nearer him than me, as I came back I met a coach with some company in't that I knew, and thought myself obliged to salute. We all lighted and met, and I found more than I looked for by two damsels and their squires. I was afterwards told they were of the Lukes, and possibly this man might be there, or else I never saw him; for since these times we have had no commerce with that family, but have kept at great distance, as having on several occasions been disobliged by them. But of late, I know not how, Sir Sam has grown so kind as to send to me for some things he desired out of this garden, and withal made the offer of what was in his, which I had reason to take for a high favour, for he is a nice florist; and since this we are insensibly come to as good degrees of civility for one another as can be expected from people that never meet.

Who those demoiselles should be that were at Heamses I cannot imagine, and I know so few that are concerned in me or my name that I admire you should meet with so many that seem to be acquainted with it. Sure, if you had liked them you would not have been so sullen, and a less occasion would have served to make you entertain their discourse if they had been handsome. And yet I know no reason I have to believe that beauty is any argument to make you like people; unless I had more on't myself. But be it what it will that displeased you, I am glad they did not fright you away before you had the orange-flower water, for it is very good, and I am so sweet with it a days that I despise roses. When I have given you humble thanks for it, I mean to look over your other letter and take the heads, and to treat of them in order as my time and your patience shall give me leave.

And first for my Sheriff,* let me desire you to believe he has more courage than to die upon a denial. No (thanks be to God!), none of my servants are given to that; I hear of many every day that marry, but of none that do worse. My brother sent me word this week that my fighting servant is married too, and with the

* Levinus Bennet, Sheriff of Cambridge. See Letters 20 and 21.

probably the prototype of Samuel Butler's 'Sir Hudibras'. He was not regarded as a friend by the Osbornes, doubtless because he was on the wrong side when Chicksands was in danger of sequestration.

news this ballad, which was to be sung in the grove that you dreamt of, I think; but because you tell me I shall not want company then, you may dispose of this piece of poetry as you please when you have sufficiently admired with me where he found it out, for 'tis much older than that of my 'Lord of Lorne.' You are altogether in the right that my brother will never be at quiet till he sees me disposed of, but he does not mean to lose me by it; he knows that if I were married at this present, I should not be persuaded to leave my father as long as he lives; and when this house breaks up, he is resolved to follow me if he can, which he thinks he might better do to a house where I had some power than where I am but upon courtesy myself. Besides that, he thinks it would be to my advantage to be well bestowed, and by that he understands richly. He is much of your sister's humour, and many times wishes me a husband that loved me as well as he does (though he seems to doubt the possibility on't), but never desires that I should love that husband with any passion, and plainly tells me so. He says it would not be so well for him, nor perhaps for me, that I should; for he is of opinion that all passions have more of trouble than satisfaction in them, and therefore they are happiest that have least of them. You think him kind from a letter that you met with of his; sure, there was very little of anything in that, or else I should not have employed it to wrap a book up. But, seriously, I many times receive letters from him, that were they seen without any address to me or his name, nobody would believe they were from a brother; and I cannot but tell him sometimes that, sure, he mistakes and sends me letters that were meant to his mistress, till he swears to me that he has none.

Next week my persecution begins again; he comes down, and my cousin Molle is already cured of his imaginary dropsy, and means to meet here. I shall be baited most sweetly, but sure they will not easily make me consent to make my life unhappy to satisfy their importunity. I was born to be very happy or very miserable, I know not which, but I am certain that as long as I am anything I shall be your most faithful friend and servant.

You will never read half this letter 'tis so scribbled; but 'tis no matter, 'tis not much worth it.

Letter 23

Dorothy tells Temple that one of his letters has arrived with the seal broken. She has blamed the carrier. She promises not to use any formalities in her letters to him. Lady Diana Rich is sitting for her portrait for Dorothy.

[SATURDAY MAY THE 28TH, 1653]

SIR, If it were the carrier's fault that you stayed so long for your letter, you are revenged, for I have chid him most unreasonably. But I must confess 'twas not for that, for I did not know it then, but going to meet him (as I usually do), when he gave me your letter I found the upper seal broke open, and underneath where it uses to be only closed with a little wax, there was a seal, which though it were an anchor and a heart, methought it did not look like yours, but less, and much worse cut. This suspicion was so strong upon me, that I chid till the poor fellow was ready to cry, and swore to me that it had never been touched since he had it, and that he was so careful of it, as he never put it with his other letters, but by itself, and that now it came amongst his money, which perhaps might break the seal; and lest I should think it was his curiosity, he told me very ingenuously he could not read, and so we parted for the present. But since, he has been with a neighbour of mine whom he sometimes delivers my letter to, and begged of her that she would go to me and desire my worship to write to your worship to know how the letter was sealed, for it has so grieved him that I should think him so dishonest that he has neither eat nor slept (to do him any good) since he came home, and in grace of God this shall be a warning to him as long as he lives. He takes it so heavily that I think I must be friends with him again; but pray hereafter seal your letters, so as the difficulty of opening them may dishearten anybody from attempting it.

It was but my guess that the ladies at Heams' were unhandsome; but since you tell me they were remarkably so, sure I know them by it; they are two sisters, and might have been mine if the Fates had so pleased. They have a brother that is not like them, and is a baronet besides. 'Tis strange that you tell me of my Lords Chandos and Arundell; but what becomes of young Compton's estate? Sure my Lady Carey cannot neither in honour nor conscience keep it; besides that, she needs it less now than ever, her son being (as I hear) dead.*

Sir Thomas, I suppose, avoids you as a friend of mine. My brother tells me they meet sometimes, and have the most ado to pull off their hats to one another that can be, and never speak. If I were in town I'll undertake he would venture the being choked for want of air rather than stir out of doors for fear of meeting me. But did not you say in your last that you took something very ill from me? Oh! 'twas my humble thanks; well, you shall have no more of them then, nor no more servants.† I think indeed that they are not necessary amongst friends.

I take it very kindly that your father asked for me, and that you were not pleased with the question he made of the continuance of my friendship. I can pardon it him, because he does not know me, but I should never forgive you if you could doubt it. Were my face in no more danger of changing than my mind, I should be worth the seeing at threescore; and that which is but very ordinary now, would then be counted handsome for an old woman; but, alas! I am more likely to look old before my time with grief. Never anybody had such luck with servants; what with marrying and what with dying, they all leave me. Just now I have news brought me of the death of an old rich knight‡ that has promised me this seven years to marry me whensoever his

* In May 1652 Lord Chandos had killed Colonel Henry Crompton in a duel on Putney Marsh. Lord Arundel had been Crompton's second. They were imprisoned and tried, and convicted of manslaughter in May 1653. Lady Carey, a natural daughter of the Earl of Sunderland, was the widow of Lord Leppington. Her son (also Lord Leppington) had just died and was buried in Westminster Abbey on May 24th, 1653. Colonel Crompton had bequeathed his estates to Lady Leppington.

† Temple has obviously complained of the way in which Dorothy ends her letters with the formal phrase 'humble servant'. She stops using the phrase and the first time we meet it again is in Letter 50, written at a time when it seemed that their relationship would never lead to marriage and would have to be discontinued.

‡ Sir William Briers of Pulloxhill, a few miles from Chicksands.

wife died, and now he's dead before her, and has left her such a widow, it makes me mad to think on't, £1,200 a year jointure and £20,000 in money and personal estate, and all this I might have had if Mr. Death had been pleased to have taken her instead of him. Well, who can help these things? But, since I cannot have him, would you have her! What say you? Shall I speak a good word for you? She will marry for certain, and though perhaps my brother may expect I should serve him in it, yet if you give me commission I'll say I was engaged beforehand for a friend, and leave him to shift for himself. You would be my neighbour if you had her, and I should see you often. Think on't, and let me know what you resolve? My lady has writ me word that she intends very shortly to sit at Lely's★ for her picture for me; I give you notice on't, that you may have the pleasure of seeing it sometimes whilst 'tis there. I imagine 'twill be so to you for I am sure it would be a great one to me, and we do not use to differ in our inclinations, though I cannot agree with you that my brother's kindness to me has anything of trouble in't; no, sure, I may be just to you and him both, and to be a kind sister will take nothing from my being a perfect friend.

Letter 24

Dorothy discusses Temple's dream of her. She then tells him about the daily round at Chicksands and gives him the latest news of her family, including her father, who seems now to be permanently bedridden.

[THURSDAY–SATURDAY JUNE THE 2ND–4TH, 1653]

SIR, I have been reckoning up how many faults you lay to my charge in your last letter, and I find I am severe, unjust, unmerciful, and unkind. Oh me, how should one do to mend all

---

★ Lady Diana Rich had her portrait painted for Dorothy in the following autumn. Peter Lely, a Dutchman, came to England in 1641 and remained throughout the Civil War, the Protectorate and the Restoration until his death in 1679. He became one of the most fashionable portrait painters of the day; Charles I and Cromwell both sat for him.

these! 'Tis work for an age, and 'tis to be feared I shall be so old before I am good, that 'twill not be considerable to anybody but myself whether I am so or not. I say nothing of the pretty humour you fancied me in, in your dream, because 'twas but a dream. Sure, if it had been anything else, I should have remembered that my Lord L. loves to have his chamber and his bed to himself. But seriously, now, I wonder at your patience. How could you hear me talk so senselessly, though 'twere but in your sleep, and not to be ready to beat me? What nice mistaken points of honour I pretend to, and yet could allow him a room in the same bed with me! Well, dreams are pleasant things to people whose humours are so; but to have the spleen and to dream upon't, is a punishment I would not wish my greatest enemy. I seldom dream, or never remember them, unless they have been so sad as to put me into such disorder as I can hardly recover when I am awake, and some of those I am confident I shall never forget.

You ask me how I pass my time here. I can give you a perfect account not only of what I do for the present, but of what I am likely to do this seven years if I stay here so long. I rise in the morning reasonably early, and before I am ready I go round the house till I am weary of that, and then into the garden till it grows too hot for me. About ten o'clock I think of making me ready, and when that's done I go into my father's chamber, from thence to dinner, where my cousin Molle and I sit in great state in a room and at a table that would hold a great many more. After dinner we sit and talk till Mr. B.* comes in question, and then I am gone. The heat of the day is spent in reading or working, and about six or seven o'clock I walk out into a common that lies hard by the house, where a great many young wenches keep sheep and cows, and sit in the shade singing of ballads. I go to them and compare their voices and beauties to some ancient shepherdesses that I have read of, and find a vast difference there; but, trust me, I think these are as innocent as those could be. I talk to them, and find they want nothing to make them the happiest people in the world but the knowledge that they are so. Most commonly, when we are in the midst of our discourse, one looks about her, and spies her cows going into the corn, and then

* Levinus Bennet, Sheriff of Cambridgeshire. See Letters 20, 21, and 22.

68

away they all run as if they had wings at their heels. I, that am not so nimble, stay behind; and when I see them driving home their cattle, I think 'tis time for me to retire too. When I have supped, I go into the garden, and so to the side of a small river that runs by it, where I sit down and wish you with me (you had best say this is not kind neither). In earnest, 'tis a pleasant place, and would be much more so to me if I had your company. I sit there sometimes till I am lost with thinking; and were it not for some cruel thoughts of the crossness of our fortunes that will not let me sleep there, I should forget that there were such a thing to be done as going to bed.

Since I writ this my company is increased by two, my brother Harry and a fair niece, the eldest of my brother Peyton's daughters.* She is so much a woman that I am almost ashamed to say I am her aunt; and so pretty, that, if I had any design to gain a servant, I should not like her company; but I have none, and therefore shall endeavour to keep her here as long as I can persuade her father to spare her, for she will easily consent to it, having so much of my humour (though it be the worst in her) as to like a melancholy place and little company. My brother John is not come down again, nor am I certain when he will be here. He went from London into Gloucestershire to my sister who was very ill, and his youngest girl, of which he was very fond, is since dead. But I believe by that time his wife has a little recovered her sickness and the loss of her child, he will be coming this way. My father is reasonably well, but keeps his chamber still, and will hardly, I am afraid, ever be so perfectly recovered as to come abroad again.

I am sorry for poor Walker,† but you need not doubt of what he has of yours in his hands, for it seems he does not use to do his work himself. I speak seriously, he keeps a Frenchman that sets all his seals and rings. If what you say of my Lady Leppington‡

---

* Dorothy Peyton, who was to be her companion for a while. Sir Thomas Peyton of Knowlton, Kent, an active Royalist, had married Dorothy's eldest sister Elizabeth. Elizabeth died in 1642 and Peyton had remarried.

† The man who had set Dorothy's seals. See Letter 13.

‡ The person that Dorothy referred to as Lady Carey in Letter 23.

be of your own knowledge, I shall believe you, but otherwise I can assure you I have heard from people that pretend to know her very well, that her kindness to Compton was very moderate, and that she never liked him so well as when he died and gave her his estate. But they might be deceived, and 'tis not so strange as that you should imagine a coldness and an indifference in my letters where I so little meant it; but I am not displeased you should desire my kindness enough to apprehend the loss of it when it is safest. Only I would not have you apprehend it so far as to believe it possible—that were an injury to all the assurances I have given you, and if you love me you cannot think me unworthy. I should think myself so, if I found you grew indifferent to me, that I have had so long and so particular a friendship for; but, sure, this is more than I need to say. You are enough in my heart to know all my thoughts, and if so, you know better than I can tell you how much I am

Yours.

Letter 25

Temple has probably mentioned his intention of going to Epsom during the summer. In this letter, and the next, Dorothy gives her reasons for not going there. Her brother Henry has returned and has suggested other suitors. She tells Temple that Sir Justinian Isham has renewed his offer of marriage and asks him for his advice in the matter.

[SATURDAY JUNE THE 11TH, 1653]

SIR, If to know I wish you with me pleases you, 'tis a satisfaction you may always have, for I do it perpetually; but were it really in my power to make you happy, I could not miss being so myself, for I know nothing else I want towards it. You are admitted to all my entertainments; and 'twould be a pleasing surprise to me to see you amongst my shepherdesses. I meet some there sometimes that look very like gentlemen (for 'tis a road), and when they are in good humour they give us a compliment as they go by; but you would be so courteous as to stay, I hope, if we entreated you; 'tis in your way to this place, and just before the house. 'Tis our Hyde Park, and every fine evening, anybody that wanted a mistress might be sure to find one there. I have wondered often to meet my fair Lady Ruthin there alone; methinks it should be dangerous for an heiress. I could find in my heart to steal her away myself, but it should be rather for her person than her fortune. My brother says not a word of you, nor your service, nor do I expect he should; if I could forget you, he would not help my memory. You would laugh, sure, if I could tell you how many servants he has offered me since he came down;* but one above all the rest I think he is in love with himself, and may marry him too if he pleases, I shall not hinder him. 'Tis one Talbot, the finest gentleman he has seen this seven year; but the mischief on't is he has not above fifteen or sixteen hundred pound a year, though he swears he begins to think one might bate £500 a year for such a husband. I tell him I am glad to hear it; and if I were as much taken (as he) with Mr. Talbot, I should not be less gallant; but I doubted the first extremely. I have spleen enough to carry me to Epsom this summer; but yet I think I shall not go. If I make one journey, I must make more, for then I have no excuse, and rather than be obliged to that, I'll make none. You have so often reproached me with the loss of your liberty, that to make you some amends I am contented to be your prisoner this summer; but you shall do one favour for me into the bargain. When your father goes into Ireland, lay your commands upon some of his servants to get you an Irish grey-hound. I have one that was the General's;† but 'tis a bitch, and those are always much less than the dogs. I got it in the time of my favour there, and it was all they had. Henry Cromwell under-took to write to his brother Fleetwood for another for me; but I have lost my hopes there. Whomsoever it is that you employ, he will need no other instructions but to get the biggest he can meet with; 'tis all the beauty of those dogs, or of any indeed, I think. A masty [mastiff] is handsomer to me than the most exact‡ little dog that ever lady played withal. You will not offer to take it ill

---

* Henry Osborne had returned to Chicksands on June 3rd, i.e. a week before this letter was written.
    † Oliver Cromwell.   ‡ Perfect.

that I employ you in such a commission, since I have told you that the General's son did not refuse it; but I shall take it ill if you do not take the same freedom whensoever I am capable of serving you. The town must needs be unpleasant now, and, methinks, you might contrive some way of having your letters sent to you without giving yourself the trouble to coming to town for them when you have no other business;* you must pardon me if I think they cannot be worth it.

I am told that R. Spencer is a servant to a lady of my acquaintance, a daughter of my Lady Lexington's. Is it true? And if it be, what is become of the £2,500 lady? Would you think it, that I have an ambassador from the Emperor Justinian that comes to renew the treaty?† In earnest, 'tis true, and I want your counsel extremely, what to do in it. You told me once that of all my servants you liked him the best. If I could do so too, there were no dispute in't. Well, I'll think on't, and if it succeed I will be as good as my word; you shall take your choice of my four daughters. Am not I beholding to him, think you? He says that he has made addresses, 'tis true, in several places since we parted, but could not fix anywhere; and, in his opinion, he sees nobody that would make so fit a wife for him as I. He has often inquired after me to hear if I were not marrying, and somebody told him I had an ague, and he presently fell sick of one too, so natural a sympathy there is between us; and yet for all this, on my conscience, we shall never marry. He desires to know whether I am at liberty or not. What shall I tell him? Or shall I send him to you to know? I think that will be best. I'll say that you are much my friend, and that I have resolved not to dispose of myself but with your consent and approbation, and therefore he must make all his court to you; and when he can bring me a certificate under your hand, that you think him a fit husband for me, 'tis very likely I may have him. Till then I am his humble servant and your faithful friend.

* Presumably Temple was still collecting Dorothy's letters from Mrs Painter in Covent Garden, but it is not known where he was living at this time.
† Sir Justinian Isham had failed to find a wife and was trying to reopen negotiations with the Osbornes for Dorothy's hand. See Letters 3 and 4.

Letter 26

Dorothy and Henry Osborne have quarrelled about Temple as a result of Sir Justinian Isham's renewed suit. They are now not on speaking terms, and Dorothy wonders how long they will continue in this way. She gives this as an added reason for not going to Epsom: she feels Henry would suspect that it was not only her spleen that drew her there.

[SATURDAY JUNE THE 18TH, 1653]

SIR, You are more in my debt than you imagine. I never deserved a long letter so much as now, when you sent me a short one. I could tell you such a story ('tis too long to be written) as would make you see (what I never discover'd in myself before) that I am a valiant lady. In earnest, we have had such a skirmish, and upon so foolish an occasion, as I cannot tell which is strangest. The Emperor and his proposals began it; I talked merrily on't till I saw my brother put on his sober face, and could hardly then believe he was in earnest. It seems he was, for when I had spoke freely my meaning, it wrought so with him as to fetch up all that lay upon his stomach. All the people that I had ever in my life refused were brought again upon the stage, like Richard the III.'s ghosts, to reproach me withal; and all the kindness his discoveries could make I had for you was laid to my charge. My best qualities (if I have any that are good) served but for aggravations of my fault, and I was allowed to have wit and understanding and discretion in other things, that it might appear I had none of this. Well, 'twas a pretty lecture, and I grew warm with it after a while; in short, we came so near an absolute falling out, that 'twas time to give over, and we said so much then that we have hardly spoken a word together since. But 'tis wonderful to see what curtseys and legs pass between us; and as before we were thought the kindest brother and sister, we are certainly now the most complimental couple* in England. 'Tis a strange change, and I am very sorry for it, but I'll swear I know not how to help it. I look upon't as one of my great misfortunes, and I must bear it, as that which is not first nor likely

* Full of formal gestures of politeness.

to be my last. 'Tis but reasonable (as you say) that you should see me, and yet I know not now how it can well be. I am not for disguises, it looks like guilt, and I would not do a thing I durst not own. I cannot tell whether (if there were a necessity of your coming) I should not choose to have it when he is at home, and rather expose him to the trouble of entertaining a person whose company (here) would not be pleasing to him, and perhaps an opinion that I did it purposely to cross him, than that your coming in his absence should be thought a concealment. 'Twas one reason more than I told you why I resolv'd not to go to Epsom this summer, because I knew he would imagine it an agreement between us, and that something besides my spleen carried me thither; but whether you see me or not you may be satisfied I am safe enough, and you are in no danger to lose your prisoner, since so great a violence as this has not broke her chains. You will have nothing to thank me for after this: my whole life will not yield such another occasion to let you see at what rate I value your friendship, and I have been much better than my word in doing but what I promised you, since I have found it a much harder thing not to yield to the power of a near relation and a great kindness, than I could then imagine it.

To let you see I did not repent me of the last commission, I'll give you another. Here is a seal that Walker set for me, and 'tis dropt out; pray give it him to mend. If anything could be wonder'd at in this age, I should very much how you come by your informations. 'Tis more than I know if Mr. Freeman* be my servant. I saw him not long since, and he told me no such thing. Do you know him? In earnest, he's a pretty gentleman, and has a great deal of good nature, I think, which may oblige him perhaps to speak well of his acquaintances without design. Mr. Fish† is the Squire of Dames, and has so many mistresses that anybody may pretend a share in him and be believed; but though I have the honour to be his near neighbour, to speak freely, I cannot brag much that he makes any court to me; and I know no young woman in the country that he does not visit oftener.

* A member of an important family living in the neighbourhood. He is mentioned in passing in a number of later letters.
† Humphrey Fyshe of Ickwell Green, not far from Chicksands.

I have sent you another tome of *Cyrus*, pray send the first to Mr. Hollingsworth for my Lady. My cousin Molle went from hence to Cambridge on Thursday, and there's an end of Mr. Bennet. I have no company now but my niece Peyton. My brother will be shortly for the term,* but will make no long stay in town. I think my youngest brother comes down with him.† Remember that you owe me a long letter and something for forgiving your last. I have no room for more than

Your.

Letter 27

Dorothy expresses herself quite firmly on the subject of gossip concerning her relationship with Temple. She is now on slightly better terms with her brother. Temple has complained of not seeing her, and she promises to have a miniature of herself made for him.

[SATURDAY JUNE THE 25TH, 1653]

SIR, You amaze me with your story of Tom Cheke.‡ I am certain he could not have it where you imagine, and 'tis a miracle to me that he remembers there is such a one in the world as his cousin D. O. I am sure he has not seen her this six year, and I think but once in his life. If he has spread his opinion in that family, I shall quickly hear on't, for my cousin Molle is now gone to Kimbolton to my Lord Manchester, and from thence he goes to Moor Park to my cousin Franklin's, and in one, or both, he will be sure to meet with it. The matter is not great, for though I confess I do naturally hate the noise and talk of the world, and should be best

* Henry Osborne left Chicksands on June 24th. The Trinity Term ended on June 29th.

† Dorothy's third brother, Robert (Robin), who died on August 26th, 1653.

‡ Although Dorothy refers to him as her cousin, the relationship was remoter than that. He was the second son of Sir Thomas Cheke, Dorothy's great-uncle by marriage. Tom Cheke's sisters were the Countess of Manchester and Mrs Richard Franklin, names that occur elsewhere in the letters.

pleased never to be known in't upon any occasion whatsoever; yet, since it can never be wholly avoided, one must satisfy oneself by doing nothing that one need care who knows. I do not think it *à propos* to tell anybody that you and I are very good friends, and it were better, sure, if nobody knew it but we ourselves. But if, in spite of all our caution, it be discovered, 'tis no treason nor anything else that's ill; and if anybody should tell me that I had a greater kindness and esteem for you than for any one besides, I do not think I should deny it; howsoever you do, oblige me by not owning any such thing, for as you say, I have no reason to take it ill that you endeavour to preserve me a liberty, though I'm never likely to make use on't. Besides that, I agree with you, too, that certainly 'tis much better you should owe my kindness to nothing but your own merit and my inclination, than that there should lie any other necessity upon me of making good my word to you.

For God sake do not complain so that you do not see me; I believe I do not suffer less in't than you, but 'tis not to be helped. If I had a picture that were fit for you, you should have it. I have but one that's anything like, and that's a great one, but I will send it some time or other to Cooper or Hoskins,* and have a little one drawn by it, if I cannot be in town to sit myself. You undo me by but dreaming how happy we might have been, when I consider how far we are from it in reality. Alas! how can you talk of defying fortune; nobody lives without it, and therefore why should you imagine you could? I know not how my brother comes to be so well informed as you say, but I am certain he knows the utmost of the injuries you have received from her.† 'Tis not possible she should have used you worse than he says. We have had another debate, but much more calmly. 'Twas just upon his going up to town, and perhaps he thought it not fit to part in anger. Not to wrong him, he never said to me (whate'er he thought) a word in prejudice of you in your own person, and I

* The portrait of her by Lely, which she proposed to send to be copied by either Samuel Cooper or John Hoskins, both fashionable miniaturists at the time.
† Dorothy is convinced that Henry Osborne knows all about Temple's financial difficulties.

never heard him accuse anything but your fortune and my indiscretion. And whereas I did expect that (at least in compliment to me) he should have said we had been a couple of fools well met, he says by his troth he does not blame you, but bids me not deceive myself to think you have any great passion for me.

If you have done with the first part of *Cyrus*, I should be glad Mr. Hollingsworth had it, because I mentioned some such thing in my last to my Lady; but there is no haste of restoring the other unless she should send to me for it, which I believe she will not. I have a third tome here against you have done with the second; and to encourage you, let me assure you that the more you read of them you will like them still better. Oh, me! whilst I think on't, let me ask you one question seriously, and pray resolve me truly—do I look so stately as people apprehend? I vow to you I made nothing on't when Sir Emperor said so, because I had no great opinion of his judgment, but Mr. Freeman makes me mistrust myself extremely, not that I am sorry I did appear so to him (since it kept me from the displeasure of refusing an offer which I do not perhaps deserve), but that it is a scurvy quality in itself, and I am afraid I have it in great measure if I showed any of it to him, for whom I have so much of respect and esteem. If it be so you must needs know it; for though my kindness will not let me look so upon you, you can see what I do to other people. And, besides, there was a time when we ourselves were indifferent to one another—did I do so then, or have I learn't it since? For God sake tell me, that I may try to mend it. I could wish, too, that you would lay your commands on me to forbear fruit; here is enough to kill 1,000 such as I am, and so excellently good, that nothing but your power can secure me; therefore forbid it me, that I may live to be.

Yours.

Letter 28

Dorothy tells Temple he must not doubt that she wants to see him. She discourses on the meaning of friendship.

SIR, In my opinion you do not understand the laws of friendship right. 'Tis generally believed it owes its birth to an agreement and conformity of humours, and that it lives no longer than 'tis preserved by the mutual care of those that bred it. 'Tis wholly governed by equality, and can there be such a thing in it, as a distinction of power? No, sure, if we are friends we must both command and both obey alike, indeed a mistress and a servant, sounds otherwise, but that is ceremony and this is truth. Yet what reason had I to furnish you with a stick to beat myself withal, or desire that you should command, that do it so severely? I must eat fruit no longer than I could be content you should be in a fever;—is not that an absolute forbidding it me? It has frightened me just now from a basket of the most tempting cherries that e'er I saw; though I know you did not mean I should eat none, but if you had I think I should have obeyed you. I am glad you lay no fault to my charge but indiscretion, though that be too much, 'tis a well-natured one in me. I confess it is a fault to believe too easily, but 'tis not out of vanity that I do it—as thinking I deserve you should love me and therefore believing it—but because I am apt to think people so honest as to speak as they mean, and the less I deserve it the more I think myself obliged. I know 'tis a fault in anyone to be mastered by a passion, and of all passions love is perhaps the least pardonable in a woman; but when 'tis mingled with gratitude 'tis sure the less to be blamed.

I do not think if there were more that loved me I should love them all, but I am certain I could not love the most perfect person in the world, unless I did first firmly believe he had a passion for me. And yet you would persuade me I am not just, because I did once in my life deny you something. I'll swear you are not, if you do not believe that next the happy end of all our wishes, I desire to see you; but you know the inconveniency that will certainly follow, and if you can dispense* with them I can, to show that my obedience is not less than yours.

I cannot hear too often that you are kind and noble enough to

* Put up with, tolerate.

prefer my interest above your own, but, sure, if I have any measure of either myself, the more liberty you give me the less I shall take. 'Tis most certain that our Emperor would have been to me rather a gaoler than a husband, and 'tis as true that (though for my own sake I think I should not make an ill wife to anybody) I cannot be a good one to any but one. I know not with what constancy* you could hear the sentence of your death, but I am certain there is nothing I could not hear with more; and if your interest in me be dearer to you than your life, it must necessarily follow that 'tis dearer to me than anything in the world besides. Therefore you may be sure I will preserve it with all my care. I cannot promise that I shall be yours because I know not how far my misfortunes may reach, nor what punishments are reserved for my fault, but I dare almost promise you shall never receive the displeasure of seeing me another's. No, in earnest, I have so many reasons to keep me from that, besides your interest, that I know not whether it be not the least of the obligations you have to me. Sure the whole world could never persuade me (unless a parent commanded it) to marry one that I had no esteem for, and where I have any, I am not less scrupulous than your father, or I should never be brought to do them the injury as to give them a wife whose affections they could never hope for; besides that, I must sacrifice myself in't and live a walking misery till the only hope that would then be left me were perfected. Oh, me! this is so sad; it has put me out of all I had to say besides. I meant to chide you for the shortness of your last letter, and to tell you that if you do not take the same liberty of telling me of all my faults I shall not think you are my friend. In earnest, 'tis true, you must use to tell me freely of anything you see amiss in me; whether I am too stately or not enough, what humour pleases you and what does not, what you would have me do and what avoid, with the same freedom that you would use to a person over whom you had an absolute power, and were concerned in. These are the laws of friendship as I understand them, and I believe I understand them right, for I am certain no one can be more perfectly a friend than I am.

Yours.

* Courage.

Letter 29

Dorothy again tells Temple that it would be unwise of him to visit Chicksands. Her brothers Henry and John have been talking a great deal about her getting married.

[SATURDAY JULY THE 9TH, 1653]

SIR, I can give you leave to doubt anything but my kindness, though I can assure you I spake as I meant when I said I had not the vanity to believe I deserv'd yours, for I am not certain whether 'tis possible for anybody to deserve that another should love them above themselves, though I am certain many may deserve it more than I. But not to dispute this with you, let me tell you that I am thus far of your opinion, that upon some natures nothing is so powerful as kindness, and that I should give that to yours which all the merit in the world besides would not draw from me. I speak as if I had not done so already; but you may choose whether you will believe me or not, for, to say truth, I do not much believe myself in that point. No, all the kindness I have or ever had is yours; nor shall I ever repent it is so, unless you shall ever repent yours. Without telling you what the inconveniences of your coming hither are, you may believe they are considerable, or else I should not deny you to myself the happiness of seeing one another; and if you dare trust me where I am equally concerned with you, I shall take hold of the first opportunity that may either admit you here or bring me nearer you. Sure you took somebody else for my cousin Peters? I can never believe her beauty able to smite anybody. I saw her when I was last in town, but she appear'd wholly the same to me, she was at St. Malo, with all her innocent good nature too, and asked for you so kindly, that I am sure she cannot have forgot you; nor do I think she has so much address as to do it merely in compliment to me. No, you are mistaken certainly; what should she do amongst all that company unless she be towards a wedding? She has been kept at home, poor soul, and suffer'd so much of purgatory in this world that she needs not fear it in the next; and yet she is as merry as ever she was, which perhaps might make

80

her look young, but that she laughs a little too much, and that will bring wrinkles, they say. Oh, me! now I talk of laughing, it makes me think of poor Jane. I had a letter from her the other day; she desired me to present her humble service to her master—she did mean you, sure, for she named everybody else that she owes any service to—and bid me say that she would keep her word with him. God knows what you have agreed on together. She tells me she shall stay long enough there to hear from me once more, and then she is resolved to come away.

Here is a seal, which pray give Walker to set for me very handsomely, and not of any of those fashions he made my others, but of something that may differ from the rest. 'Tis a plain head, but not ill cut, I think. My eldest brother is now here, and we expect my youngest shortly, and then we shall be all together, which I do not think we ever were twice in our lives. My niece is still with me, but her father threatens to fetch her away. If I can keep her to Michaelmas I may perhaps bring her up to town myself, and take that occasion of seeing you; for I have no other business that is worth my taking a journey for. I have had another summons from my aunt,* and I protest I am afraid I shall be in rebellion there; but 'tis not to be helped. The widow† writes me word, too, that I must expect her here about a month hence; and I find that I shall want no company, but only that which I would have, and for which I could willingly spare all the rest. Will it be ever thus? I am afraid it will. There has been complaints made on me already to my eldest brother (only in general, or at least he takes notice of no more), what offers I refuse, and what a strange humour has possessed me of being deaf to the advice of all my friends. I find I am to be baited by them all by turns. They weary themselves, and me too, to very little purpose, for to my thinking they talk the most impertinently that ever people did; and I believe they are not in my debt, but think the same of me. Sometimes I tell them I will not marry, and then they laugh at me; sometimes I say, 'Not yet,' and then they laugh more, and would make me believe I shall be old within this twelvemonth. I

* Lady Gargrave, with whom Dorothy had stayed in London earlier in the year.
† Mrs Thorold. See Letter 10.

tell them I shall be wiser then. They say 'twill be then to no purpose. Sometimes we are in earnest and sometimes in jest, but always saying something since my brother Harry found his tongue again. If you were with me I could make sport of all this; but 'patience is my penance' is somebody's motto, and I think it must be mine. I am

Yours.

Letter 30

Dorothy tells Temple of her brother's attempts to intercept her letters. She has more to say on the subject of friendship.

[SATURDAY JULY THE 16TH, 1653]

SIR, I received your last sooner by a day than I expected. It was not the less welcome, but the carrier was who brought me none. I admired at myself to remember how I have been transported with the sight of that pitiful fellow, and now that I knew that he had no letter for me how coldly I looked upon him. Nan tells me* he had the curiosity to ask your boy questions. I should never have expected it. And yet he had the wit to do a thing last week few such people would have done. My brother coming from London met him going up and called to him and asked what letters he had of mine. The fellow said none, I did not use to send by him. My brother said I told him he had, and bid him call for them. He said there was some mistake in't for he had none, and so they parted for awhile. But my brother not satisfied with this, rides after him and in some anger threatened the poor fellow, who would not be frighted out of his letter, but looked very simply and said now he remembered himself, he had carried a letter for me about a fortnight or three weeks agone to my lady Diana Rich, but he was sure he had none now. My brother smiled at his innocence and left him, and I was hugely pleased to

* We generally hear of Nan Stacy in London, and the news mentioned here definitely comes from London. She must have sent it by letter or have been visiting in the neighbourhood of Chicksands. See Letter 15.

hear how he had been defeated. You will have time enough to think of a new address. He goes no more till after harvest, and you will receive this by your old friend Collins. But because my brother is with him every week as soon as he comes, and takes up all the letters, if you please let yours be made up in some other form than usual and directed to Mr. Edward Gibson* at Chicksands in some odd hand, and be at the charge pray of buying a two-penny seal a purpose on these letters.

Would you could make your own words good, that my eyes can dispel all melancholy cloudy humours; I would look in the glass all day long but I would clear up mine own. Alas they are so far from that, they would teach one to be sad that knew nothing on't, for in other people's opinion as well as my own, they have the most on't in them that eyes can have. My mother, I remember, used to say I needed no tears to persuade my troubles, and that I had looked so far beyond them, that were all the friends I had in the world dead, more could not be expected than such sadness in my eye. This indeed is natural to them or at least long custom has made it so.

'Tis most true that our friendship has been brought up hardly enough, and possibly it thrives the better for't, 'tis observed that surfeits kill more than fasting does, but our's is in no danger of that. My brother would persuade me there is no such thing in the world as a constant friendship. People, he says, that marry with great passion for one another, as they think, come afterwards to lose it they know not how, besides the multitude of such as are false and mean it. I cannot be of his opinion, though I confess there are too many examples on't. I have always believed there might be a friendship perfect like that you describe, and methinks I find something like it in myself. But sure 'tis not to be taught, it must come naturally to those that have it, and those who have it not can ne'er be made to understand it.

You needed not have feared that I should take occasion from your not answering my last not to write this week. You are as

* The Rev. Edward Gibson, vicar of Hawnes. He was probably un-married at the time, and is mentioned later in the letters as having had long evening talks with Henry Osborne. Henry's diary indicates that Gibson may have been staying at Chicksands at this time.

much pleased, you say, with writing to me as I can be to receive your letters. Why should you not think the same of me? In earnest you may, and if you love me you will, but then how much more satisfied should I be if there were no need of these and we might talk all that we write and more. Shall we ever be so happy?

Last night I was in the garden till 11 o'clock. It was the sweetest night that e'er I saw. The garden looked so well and the jasmine smelt beyond all perfume. And yet I was not pleased. The place had all the charms it used to have when I was most satisfied with it, and had you been there I should have liked it much more than ever I did; but that not being, it was no more to me than the next field, and only served me for a place to roam in without disturbance.

What a sad story you tell me of the little Marquise.* Poor woman! Yet she's happy, she's dead. For sure her life could not be very pleasing to her. When we were both girls I had a great acquaintance there, they lived by us at Chelsea, and as long as his son lived Sir Theodore did me the honor to call me daughter. But whilst I was first in France he died, and with him my converse with the family. For though my mother had occasion to be often there yet I went very seldom with her, they were still so passionate for their son that I never failed of setting them all a crying, and then I was no company for them. But this poor lady had a greater loss of my Lord Hastings who died just when they should have been married, and sure she could not think she had recovered it at all by marrying this buffle-headed† Marquis. And yet one knows not neither what she might think. I remember I saw her with him in the park a little while after they were married, and she kissed him the kindliest that could be in the midst of all the company. I shall never wish to see a worse sight than 'twas, nor to be anything longer than I am

Your faithful.

---

* Elizabeth, daughter of the famous physician Sir Theodore de Mayerne, and wife of Pierre de Caumont, Marquis de Cugnac. She died in 1653, and there is a monument to her in Chelsea church. As Elizabeth de Mayerne she had been betrothed to Lord Hastings, who had died on the eve of the wedding at the age of nineteen.

† Stupid.

84

Letter 31

Dorothy has more to say about the attempts of her brother Henry to ascertain the real nature of her relationship with Temple. She gives a not unsympathetic picture of her eldest brother John, whose attitude to the friendship is more human than Henry's.

[SATURDAY JULY THE 23RD, 1653]

SIR, Your last came safe, and I shall follow your direction for the address of this, though, as you say, I cannot imagine what should tempt anybody to so severe a search for them, unless it be that he★ is not yet fully satisfied to what degree our friendship is grown, and thinks he may best inform himself from them. In earnest, 'twould not be unpleasant to hear our† discourses. He forms his with so much art and design, and is so pleased with the hopes of making some discovery, and I that know him as well as he does himself, cannot but give myself the recreation some-times of confounding him and destroying all that his busy head had been working on since the last conference. He gives me some trouble with his suspicions; yet, on my conscience, he is a greater to himself, and I deal with so much *franchise*‡ as to tell him so many times; and yet he has no more the heart to ask me directly what he would so fain know, than a jealous man has to ask (one that might tell him) whether he were a cuckold or not, for fear of being resolved of that which is yet a doubt to him. My eldest brother is not so inquisitive; he satisfies himself with persuading me earnestly to marry, and takes no notice of anything that may hinder me, but a carelessness of my fortune, or perhaps an aversion to a kind of life that appears to have less of freedom in't than that which I at present enjoy. But, sure, he gives himself another reason, for 'tis not very long since he took occasion to inquire for you very kindly of me; and though I could then give but little account of you, he smiled as if he did not altogether believe me, and afterwards maliciously said he wondered you did not marry. I seemed to do so too, and said, if I knew any woman

★ Henry Osborne.   † The conversations between Dorothy and Henry.
‡ Freedom of speech, frankness.

85

that had a great fortune, and were a person worthy of you, I should wish her you with all my heart. 'But, sister,' says he, 'would you have him love her?' 'Do you doubt it?' would I say; 'he were not happy in't else.' He laughed, and said my humour was pleasant; but he made some question whether it was natural or not. He cannot be so unjust as to let me lose him, sure, I was kinder to him though I had some reasons not to take it very well when he made that a secret to me which was known to so many that did not know him;* but we shall never fall out, I believe, we are not apt to it, neither of us.

If you are come back from Epsom, I may ask you how you like drinking water? I have wished it might agree as well with you as it did with me; and if it were as certain that the same things would do us good as 'tis that the same things would please us, I should not need to doubt it. Otherwise my wishes do not signify much, but I am forbid complaints, or to express my fears. And be it so, only you must pardon me if I cannot agree to give you false hopes; I must be deceived myself before I can deceive you, and I have so accustomed myself to tell you all that I think, that I must either say nothing, or that which I believe to be true.

I cannot say but that I have wanted Jane; but it has been rather to have somebody to talk with of you, than that I needed anybody to put me in mind of you, and with all her diligence I should have often prevented† her in that discourse. Were you at Althorp‡ when you saw my Lady Sunderland and Mr. Smith, or are they in town? I have heard, indeed, that they are very happy; but withal that, as she is a very extraordinary person herself, so she aims at doing extraordinary things, and when she had married Mr. Smith (because some people were so bold as to think she did it because she loved him) she undertook to convince the world that what she had done was in mere pity to his sufferings,

---

* I did not bring up the subject of his marriage, though I had been hurt by his not taking me into his confidence about it when so many other people knew.
† Anticipated.
‡ Althorpe, Northants, the seat of the Spencers, to which Lady Sunderland had taken her new husband, Mr Robert Smith. See Letter 6.

and that she could not go a step lower to meet anybody than that led her, though where she thought there were no eyes upon her, she was more gracious to him. But perhaps this might not be true, or it may be she is now grown weary of that constraint she put upon herself. I should have been sadder than you if I had been their neighbour to have seen them so kind; as I must have been if I had married the Emperor.* He used to brag to me always of a great acquaintance he had there, what an esteem my lady had for him, and had the vanity (not to call it impudence) to talk sometimes as if he would have had me believe he might have had her, and would not; I'll swear I blushed for him when I saw he did not. He told me too, that though he had carried his addresses to me with all the privacy that was possible, because he saw I liked it best, and that 'twas partly his own humour too, yet she had discovered it, and could tell that there had been such a thing, and that it was broke off again, she knew not why; which certainly was a lie, as well as the other, for I do not think she ever heard there was such a one in the world
as your faithful friend.

Letter 32

Temple has returned from Epsom, and Dorothy comments on the waters there and his complaint. She tells him an amusing story about a visit she and her brother had paid to a newly married couple in the neighbourhood.

[SATURDAY AUGUST THE 5TH, 1653]

SIR, I did not lay it as a fault to your charge that you were not good at disguise; if it be one, I am too guilty on't myself to accuse another. And though I have been told it shows an unpractisedness in the world, and betrays one to all that understand it better, yet since it is a quality I was not born with, nor ever

---

* Sir Justinian Isham. If Dorothy had married him, she would have lived at Lamport, about seven miles from Althorpe, and so been neighbours of Lady Sunderland and her new husband.

like to get, I have always thought good to maintain that it was better not to need it than to have it.

I give you many thanks for your care of my Irish dog,* but I am extremely out of countenance your father should be troubled with it. Sure, he will think I have a most extravagant fancy; but do me the right as to let him know I am not so possessed with it as to consent he should be employed in such a commission.

Your opinion of my eldest brother is, I think, very just, and when I said maliciously, I meant a French malice, which you know does not signify the same with an English one. I know not whether I told it you or not, but I concluded (from what you said of your indisposition) that it was very like the spleen; but perhaps I foresaw you would not be willing to own a disease that the severe part of the world holds to be merely imaginary and affected, and therefore proper only to women. However, I cannot but wish you had stayed longer at Epsom and drunk the waters with more order though in a less proportion. But did you drink them immediately from the well? I remember I was forbid it, and methought with a great deal of reason, for (especially at this time of year) the well is so low, and there is such a multitude to be served out on't, that you can hardly get any but what is thick and troubled; and I have marked that when it stood all night (for that was my direction) the bottom of the vessel it stood in would be covered an inch thick with a white clay, which, sure, has no great virtue in't, and is not very pleasant to drink.

What a character of a young couple you give me! Would you would ask somebody that knew him, whether he be not much more an ass since his marrying than he was before. I have some reasons to doubt that it alters people strangely. I made a visit t'other day† to welcome a lady into this country whom her husband has newly brought down, and because I knew him, though not her, and she was a stranger here, 'twas a civility I owed them. But you cannot imagine how I was surprised to see

* Dorothy reminds Temple of a request she had made earlier (Letter 25) that Sir John Temple should obtain an Irish greyhound for her. Sir John was about to leave for Ireland at this time.

† Dorothy is reminded by Temple's story of a visit she and Henry had paid the Hillesdens of Elstow, a few miles from Chicksands.

a man that I had known so handsome, so capable of being made a pretty gentleman (for though he was no *grand Philosophe,* as the Frenchmen say, yet he was that which good company and a little knowledge of the world would have made equal to many that think themselves very well, and are thought so), transformed into the direct shape of a great boy newly come from school. To see him wholly taken up with running on errands for his wife, and teaching her little dog tricks! And this was the best of him; for when he was at leisure to talk, he would suffer nobody else to do it, and by what he said, and the noise he made, if you had heard it, you would have concluded him drunk with joy that he had a wife and a pack of hounds. I was so weary on't that I made haste home, and could not but think of the change all the way till my brother (who was with me) thought me sad, and to put me in better humour, said he believed I repented me I had not this gentleman, now I saw how absolutely his wife governed him. But I assured him, that though I thought it very fit such as he should be governed, yet I should not like the employment by no means. It became no woman, and did so ill with this lady that in my opinion it spoiled a good face and a very fine gown. Yet the woman you met upon the way governed her husband and did it handsomely. It was, as you say, a great example of friendship, and much for the credit of our sex.

You are too severe to Walker. I'll undertake he would set me twenty seals for nothing rather than undergo your wish. I am in no haste for it, and so he does it well we will not fall out; perhaps he is not in the humour of keeping his word at present, and nobody can blame him if he be often in an ill one. But though I am merciful to him, as to one that has suffered enough already, I cannot excuse you that profess to be my friend and yet are content to let me live in such ignorance, write to me every week, and yet never send me any of the phrases of the town. I could tell you without abandoning the truth, that it is part of your *devoyre* to correct the imperfections you find under my hand, and that my trouble resembles my wonder you can let me be dissatisfied. I should never have learnt any of these fine things from you; and, to say truth, I know not whether I shall from anybody else, if to learn them be to understand them. Pray what is meant by *wellness* and *unwellness*; and why is *to some extreme* better than *to some extremity*? I believe I shall live here till there is quite a new language spoke where you are★ and shall come out like one of the Seven Sleepers,† a creature of another age. But 'tis no matter so you understand me, though nobody else do, when I say how much I am

Your faithful.

Letter 33

Jane, Dorothy's friend and companion, has returned from Guernsey. Dorothy tells Temple of her intention to find some opportunity for coming to London. She reflects on the length of time they have known one another.

[FRIDAY AUGUST THE 12TH, 1653]

SIR, Jane was so unlucky as to come out of town before your return, but she tells me she left my letter with Nan Stacy for you. I was in hope she would have brought me one from you; and because she did not I was resolv'd to punish her, and kept her up till one o'clock telling me all her stories. Sure, if there be any truth in the old observation, your cheeks glowed notably; and 'tis most certain that if I were with you, I should chide notably. What do you mean to be so melancholy? By her report your humour is grown insupportable. I can allow it not to be altogether what she says, and yet it may be very ill too; but if you loved me you would not give yourself over to that which will infallibly kill you, if it continue. I know too well that our

★ Temple has obviously commented on some expressions used by Dorothy and she finds some that he has suggested unknown or strange to her. It is interesting to notice that about this time Dorothy's spelling began to improve, as though Temple had commented on it. This is apparent from the MSS of the letters.

† Seven young men who had fled from Ephesus to avoid an edict of the Emperor Decius and hidden in a cave. Decius ordered all caves to be sealed up. This was in the year AD 250. In 479 they are supposed to have appeared, under the impression that they had slept for one night. The legend also appears in the Koran.

fortunes have given us occasion enough to complain and to be weary of her tyranny; but, alas! would it be better if I had lost you or you me; unless we were sure to die both together, 'twould but increase our misery, and add to that which is more already than we can well tell how to bear. You are more cruel than she in hazarding a life that's dearer to me than that of the whole world's besides, and which makes all the happiness I have or ever shall be capable of. Therefore, by all our friendship I conjure you and, by the power you have given me, command you, to preserve yourself with the same care that you would have me live. 'Tis all the obedience I require of you, and will be the greatest testimony you can give me of your faith. When you have promised me this, 'tis not impossible but I may promise you shall see me shortly; though my brother Peyton (who says he will come down to fetch his daughter) hinders me from making the journey in compliment to her. Yet I shall perhaps find business enough to carry me up to town. 'Tis all the service I expect from two girls whose friends have given me leave to provide for, that some order I must take for the disposal of them may serve for my pretence to see you; but then I must find you pleased and in good humour, merry as you were wont to be when we first met, if you will not have me show that I am nothing akin to my cousin Osborne's lady.*

But what an age 'tis since we first met, and how great a change it has wrought in both of us; if there had been as great a one in my face, it would be either very handsome or very ugly. For God sake, when we meet, let us design one day to remember old stories in, to ask one another by what degrees our friendship grew to this height 'tis at. In earnest, I am lost sometimes with thinking on't; and though I can never repent the share you have in my heart, I know not whether I gave it you willingly or not at first. No, to speak ingenuously, I think you got an interest there a good while before I thought you had any, and it grew so insensibly, and yet so fast, that all the traverses† it has met with

* Dorothy's cousin Sir Thomas Osborne had recently married Lady Bridget Bertie, daughter of the Earl of Lindsey. Temple knew Osborne, and had probably mentioned Lady Bridget in his last letter.
† Obstacles.

since has served rather to discover* it to me than at all to hinder it. By this confession you will see I am past all disguise with you, and that you have reason to be satisfied with knowing as much of my heart as I do myself. Will the kindness of this letter excuse the shortness on't? Pray let it! For I have twenty more, I think, to write, and the hopes I had of receiving one from you last night kept me from writing this when I had more time; or if all this will not satisfy, make your own conditions, so you do not return it me by the shortness of yours. Your servant† kisses your hands, and I am

Your faithful.

FOR MR. T.
LET THE ANSWER BE SENT BY HARROLD.

Letter 34

Dorothy has read Temple's letter to his brother. She reflects further on the length of their friendship and the effect of time on her looks. Temple has told her that his father remembers her with kindness; she asks whether Temple has praised her to him.

[SATURDAY AUGUST THE 20TH, 1653]

SIR, You cannot imagine how I was surpris'd to find a letter that began 'Dear brother;'‡ I thought sure it could not belong at all to me, and was afraid I had lost one by it; that you intended me another, and in your haste had mistook this for that. Therefore, till I found the permission you gave me, I had laid it by with a resolution not to read it, but to send it again. If I had done so, I had missed of a great deal of satisfaction which I received from it. In earnest, I cannot tell how kindly I take all the obliging things you say in it of me; nor how pleased I should be (for your sake) if I were able to make good§ the character you give of me to your brother, and that I did not owe a great part of it wholly

* Reveal. † Jane Wright.
‡ This was undoubtedly William's elder brother John. His younger brother, Henry, was only fifteen at the time.
§ To justify.

to your friendship for me. I dare call nothing on't my own but faithfulness; that I may boast of with truth and modesty, since 'tis but a single virtue; and though some are without it, yet 'tis so absolutely necessary, that nobody wanting it can be worthy of any esteem. I see you speak well of me to other people, though you complain always to me. I know not how to believe I should misuse your heart as you pretend; I never had any quarrel to it, and since our friendship it has been dear to me as my own. 'Tis rather, sure, that you have a mind to try another, than that any dislike of yours makes you turn it over to me; but be it as it will, I am contented to stand to the loss, and perhaps when you have changed you will find so little difference that you'll be calling for your own again. Do but assure me that I shall find you almost as merry as my Lady Anne Wentworth is always, and nothing shall fright me from my purpose of seeing you as soon as I can with any conveniency. I would not have you insensible of our misfortunes, but I would not neither that you should revenge them upon yourself; no, that shows a want of constancy* (which you will hardly yield to be your fault); but 'tis certain that there was never anything more mistaken than the Roman courage, when they killed themselves to avoid misfortunes that were infinitely worse than death. You confess 'tis an age since our story began, as is not fit for me to own. Is it not likely, then, that if my face had ever been good, it might be altered since then; or is it as unfit for me to own the change as the time that makes it? Be it as you please, I am not enough concerned in't to dispute it with you; for, trust me, if you would not have me face better, I am satisfied that it should be as it is; since if I ever wished it otherwise, 'twas for your sake.

I know not how I stumbled upon a news-book† this week, and, for want of something else to do read it; it mentions my Lord Lisle's embassage again. Is there any such thing towards? I met with somebody else too in't that may concern anybody that has a mind to marry; 'tis a new form for it,‡ that, sure, will

---

* Courage.   † The contemporary description of a newspaper.

‡ i.e. marriage. After he had dissolved the Rump Parliament, Cromwell summoned a total of 128 men to Westminster from all parts of England, Scotland, and Ireland to act as a legislature. On August 24th this body,

fright the country people extremely, for they apprehend nothing like going before a Justice; they say no other marriage shall stand good in law. In conscience, I believe the old one is the better; and for my part I am resolved to stay till that comes in fashion again.

Can your father have so perfectly forgiven already the injury I did him (since you will not allow it to be any to you), in hindering you of Mrs. Cl.,* as to remember me with kindness? 'Tis most certain that I am obliged to him, and, in earnest, if I could hope it might ever be in my power to serve him I would promise something for myself. But is it not true, too, that you have represented me to him rather as you imagine me than as I am; and have you not given him an expectation that I shall never be able to satisfy? If you have, I can forgive you, because I know you meant well in it; but I have known some women that have commended others merely out of spite, and if I were malicious enough to envy anybody's beauty, I would cry it up to all that had not seen them; there's no such way to make anybody appear less handsome than they are.

You must not forget that you are some letters in my debt, besides the answer to this. If there were more conveniences of sending, I should persecute you strangely. And yet you cannot wonder at it; the constant desire I have to hear from you, and the satisfaction your letters give me, would oblige one that has less time to write often. But yet I know what 'tis to be in the town. I could never write a letter from thence in my life of above a dozen lines; and though I see as little company as anybody that comes there, yet I always met with something or other that kept me idle. Therefore I can excuse it, though you do not exactly pay all that you owe, upon condition you shall tell me when I see you all that you should have writ if you had had time, and all that you can imagine to say to a person that is

Your faithful friend.

* See Letter 10.

---

having voted itself a Parliament, passed an act which made marriages legal only when performed before a Justice of the Peace. This was the only piece of legislation that the Assembly effected before it resigned its powers into Cromwell's hands.

Letter 35

Temple has said that her letters are his only happiness. She says she is too great a 'friend' to become his mistress.

[SATURDAY AUGUST THE 27TH, 1653]

SIR, 'Tis most true that I could not excuse it to myself if I should not write to you, and that I owe it to my own satisfaction as well as to yours, or rather 'tis a pleasure to me because 'tis acceptable to you. But I cannot think it deserves that you should quit all other entertainment and leave yourself nothing to be happy in but that which is an effect of the absence you complain of, and that which, if we were but a little more happy, we should quickly despise. At the same time that my letters tell you I am well, and still your friend, they tell you too that I am where you cannot see me, and where I vainly wish you, and when they are kindest and most welcome to you, they only show that 'tis impossible I should desire your happiness more or have less power to make it. You shall not persuade me to be your mistress if you would, I am too much your friend to act that part well. I knew a lady that rather than she would want an occasion to be cruel made it a fault in her servant that he loved her too much, and another, that her's was not jealous of her. Sure they foresee their reigns are to be but short, and that makes them such tyrants.

I heard a good while agone that my lady Udall* was resolved to marry a kind man that lived in the house with her, and methought 'twas an odd story then. But since you tell me he has been in love with her seventeen years, it appears stranger to me a great deal. For if she did not love him what could persuade her to marry him, and if she did, in my opinion she made him but an ill requital for seventeen years' service to marry him when she had spent all her youth and beauty with another. She was handsome enough once, or else some picture that I have seen of

* Second wife of Sir William Udall, or Uvedale. He had a son, William, by his first wife. This son had died shortly before his second marriage. Sir William died in December 1652. His widow married a Bartholomew Price of Wickham, Hants, on August 14th, 1653.

her flatters her very much; that and her wit together got her so many servants that they hindered one another and her too, I think. Sir William Udall and his son were rivals and (which was stranger) she pleased them both; the son thought himself sure of her as long as he lived, and the father knew he might have her when his son was dead.

This word 'dead' makes me remember to ask you a question that I have forgot twice or thrice. They say my Lady St. John* is dead in child-bed; is it true or not? If it be, Mrs. Freschville is nearer being mad than ever she was in her life. To lose such a daughter and eight thousand pound is more than her head can bear. 'Twas the younger Mrs. Bishop† that was counted like me, but when that was, she was not thought a beauty; for her eldest sister (who in my judgment had no excuse on't either) was esteemed the handsomer in those days. But a year or two mends some as much as it impairs others, and she may have now outgrown what she had of like me to her advantage; but 'tis most certain that we have something of likeness in our humours still, for I should have made the same ingenuous confession that she did, if I had been put to it, and Mr. Heningham's‡ four thousand a year would have tempted me as little. Lord! I would not be so perplexed for the whole world, as that poor man is where to find a wife that may be young and handsome and that he may be secure in. For he says: 'She must be a very sweet natured lady, or else he is in danger of dying as meritoriously as the good husband you mention that hanged himself.' 'Twere no great loss, I think (as you say), if his brain were broke as well as his heart, but for a man that has no more wit he is the fullest of caution that I have heard of. A 'Sir Justinian' could not be more wary in his choice. And to say truth they are much in a condition, and have both the same hopes and fears, only the last has something the better opinion of himself and is therefore the more likely to be deceived.

* Christian, eldest daughter of John Freschville, who later became Lord Freschville of Stavely Musard and Fitzralph, had married Charles Powlett, Lord St John. She died on July 22nd, 1653.

† Probably one of the daughters of Sir Edward Bishop of Parham, Sussex.

‡ He appears several times in the letters: as a suitor of Dorothy's neighbour Lady Grey de Ruthin in Letter 44, and as having been suggested as a suitable husband for Dorothy herself.

I had a letter the last week from my Lady, who tells me that she has been ill from a pain at her stomach, and that she has been drinking Barnet Waters and has found herself better since. I thought they had been so lately found out, that nobody had known what they had been good for yet, or had ventured to take them. I could wish they were as proper for the spleen as Epsom or Tunbridge, they would lie much more conveniently for me. Besides that I have no more heart to go to Epsom since Sir Robert Cook died.* Ah! that good old man, I would so fain have had him, but I have no luck to them, they all die. If he would have married me first and then have died 'twould not have grieved me half so much as it does now. Yet I was offered a new servant, t'other day and after two hours talk, and that they had told me that he had as good as two thousand pounds a year in present, and a thousand more to come, I had not the curiosity to ask who 'twas, which they took so ill that I think I shall hear no more on't. Never man made a worse bargain than you did, when you played for the ten pounds I am to pay when I marry.† In conscience now what would you give me to be quit on't? Because you shall see I am your friend, I will release you for a favour at your wedding, but you must keep your own counsel then, for there are a great many others whom I have at the same advantage that must not expect to be so favourably used. My paper has not dealt so well with me, I thought I had half a side good still, but I see I must make an end in earnest and say I am

Your faithful.

Letter 36

Dorothy accuses Temple of dissembling, and asks him to use 'plainheartedness' in his letters to her. She is in mourning for her brother Robin. She discusses the marriage of General Monk.

* Also spelled Coke or Cooke, son of Sir Edward Coke, Lord Chief Justice during the reign of Queen Elizabeth, and married to Theophilia, sister of Lord Berkeley. She died in 1643, and Dorothy had probably seen much of Sir Robert when she was at Epsom in 1652.

† See Letter 1.

SIR, It was, sure, a less fault in me to make a scruple of reading your letter to your brother, which in all likelihood I could not be concerned in, than for you to condemn the freedom you take of giving me directions in a thing where we are equally concerned. Therefore, if I forgive you this, you may justly forgive me t'other; and upon these terms we are friends again, are we not? No, stay! I have another fault to chide you for. You doubted whether you had not writ too much, and whether I could have the patience to read it or not. Why do you dissemble so abominably; you cannot think these things? How I should love that plain-heartedness you speak of, if you would use it; nothing is civil but that amongst friends. Your kind sister ought to chide you, too, for not writing to her, unless you have been with her to excuse it. I hope you have; and pray take some time to make her one visit from me, carry my humble service with you, and tell her that 'tis not my fault that you are no better. I do not think I shall see the town before Michaelmas, therefore you may make what sallies you please. I am tied here to expect my brother Peyton, and then possibly we may go up together, for I should be at home again before the term.* Then I may show you my niece; and you may confess that I am a kind aunt to desire her company, since the disadvantage of our being together will lie wholly upon me. But I must make it in my bargain, that if I come you will not be frighted to see me; you think, I'll warrant, you have courage enough to endure a worse sight. You may be deceived, you never saw me in mourning yet†; nobody that has will e'er desire to do it again, for their own sakes as well as mine. Oh, 'tis a most dismal dress—I have not dared to look in the glass since I wore it; and certainly if it did so ill with other people as it does with me, it would never be worn.

You told me of writing to your father,‡ but you did not say whether you had heard from him, or how he did. May not I ask

* Michaelmas term, which began on October 23rd. Dorothy arrived in London on October 28th.

† We learn from Henry Osborne's diary that his brother Robin had died on August 26th.

‡ Sir John Temple had left London, probably for Ireland.

it? Is is possible that he saw me?* Where were my eyes that I did not see him, for I believe I should have guessed at least 'twas he if I had? They say you are very like him; but 'tis no wonder neither that I did not see him, for I saw not you when I met you there. 'Tis a place I look upon nobody in; and it was reproached to me by a kinsman, but a little before you came to me, that he had followed me to half a dozen shops to see when I would take notice of him, and was at last going away with a belief 'twas not I, because I did not seem to know him. Other people make it so much their business to gape, that I'll swear they put me so out of countenance I dare not look up for my life.

I am sorry for General Monk's† misfortune, because you say he is your friend; but otherwise she will suit well enough with the rest of the great ladies of the times, and become Greenwich as well as some others do the rest of the King's houses. If I am not mistaken, that Monk has a brother lives in Cornwall,‡ an honest gentleman, I have heard, and one that was a great acquaintance of a brother of mine§ who was killed there during the war, and so much his friend that upon his death he put himself and his family into mourning for him, which is not usual, I think, where there is no relation of kindred.

I will take order that my letters shall be left with Jones, and yours called for there. As long as your last was, I read it over thrice in less than an hour, though, to say truth, I had skipped some on't the last time. I could not read my own confession so often. Love is a terrible word, and I should blush to death if

* Sir John had probably told William that he had seen Dorothy in a shop in London.

† The secret marriage of General Monk to Anne Clarges had just been revealed. Anne was a woman of low birth who had been Monk's sempstress, and mistress, for some time. Monk was in sole command of the fleet at the time, and Greenwich Palace was his official residence. Pepys says that Anne 'became the laughing stock of the court, and gave general disgust'. She died as the Duchess of Albemarle.

‡ Nicholas Monk, who had been rector of Langtree, near Torrington, Devon.

§ Charles Osborne. It was near Torrington (see note ‡ above) that Fairfax defeated the Royalist army, establishing the power of the Parliament in the west. Charles Osborne fell in this fighting.

anything but a letter accused me on't. Pray be merciful, and let it run friendship in my next charge. My Lady sends me word she has received those parts of *Cyrus* I lent you. Here is another for you which, when you have read, you know how to dispose. There are four pretty stories in it, '*L'Amant Absent,*' '*L'Amant non Aymé,*' '*L'Amant Jaloux,*' et '*L'Amant dont La Maitresse est mort.*' Tell me which you have most compassion for. When you have read what every one says for himself, perhaps you will not think it so easy to decide which is the most unhappy, as you may think by the titles their stories bear. Only let me desire you not to pity the jealous one, for I remember I could do nothing but laugh at him as one that sought his own vexation. This, and the little journeys (you say) you are to make, will entertain you till I come; which, sure, will be as soon as possible I can, since 'tis equally desired by you and your faithful.

Letter 37

Dorothy discusses Le Grand Cyrus, *which she has sent to Temple. She sends good wishes for Sir John Temple's safe passage to Ireland.*

[SEPTEMBER 1653]

SIR, All my quarrels to you are kind ones, for, sure, 'tis alike impossible for me to be angry as for you to give me the occasion; therefore, when I chide (unless it be that you are not careful enough of yourself, and hazard too much a health that I am more concerned in than in my own), you need not study much for excuses, I can easily forgive you anything but want of kindness. The judgment you have made of the four lovers I recommended to you does so perfectly agree with what I think of them, that I hope it will not alter when you have read their stories. *L'Amant Absent* has (in my opinion) a mistress so much beyond any of the rest, that to be in danger of losing her is more than to have lost the others; *L'Amant non Aimé* was an ass, under favour★ (notwithstanding the *Princesse Cleobuline*'s letter); his mistress had

★ I speak under correction.

100

caprices that would have suited better with our *Amant Jaloux* than with anybody else; and the *Prince Artibie* was much to blame that he outlived his *belle Leontine*. But if you have met with the beginning of the story of *Amestris and Aglatides*, you will find the rest of it in this part I send you now; and 'tis, to me, one of the prettiest I have read, and the most natural. They say the gentleman that writes this romance has a sister* that lives with him, a maid, and she furnishes him with all the little stories that come between, so that he only contrives the main design; and when he wants something to entertain his company withal, he calls to her for it. She has an excellent fancy, sure, and a great deal of wit; but, I am sorry to tell it you, they say 'tis the most ill-favoured creature that ever was born. And it is often so; how seldom do we see a person excellent in anything but they have some great defect with it that pulls them low enough to make them equal with other people, and there is justice in't. Those that have fortunes have nothing else, and those that want it deserve to have it. That's but small comfort, though, you'll say; 'tis confessed, but there is no such thing as perfect happiness in this world, those that have come the nearest it had many things to wish; and—bless me, whither am I going? Sure, 'tis the death's head I see before me puts me into this grave discourse (pray do not think I meant that for a conceit neither); how idly have I spent two sides of my paper, and am afraid, besides, I shall not have time to write two more. Therefore I'll make haste to tell you that my friendship for you makes me concerned in all your relations; that I have a great respect for Sir John, merely as he is your father, and that 'tis much increased by his kindness to you; that he has all my prayers and wishes for his safety; and that you will oblige me in letting me know when you hear any good news from him. He has met with a great deal of good company, I believe. My Lady Ormonde,† I am told, is waiting for a

* See Letter 20.

† The Earl of Ormonde had been Lord-Lieutenant of Ireland and had defended the Royalist cause there. He fled to France and was living there in great poverty. Lady Ormonde went to England in 1652 to claim the portion of their estates that had originally been hers. She had just been granted permission to cross to Ireland. Eventually she was granted £500 and an allowance from estates in Galway.

passage, and divers others; but this wind (if I am not mistaken) is not good for them. In earnest, 'tis a most sad thing that a person of her quality should be reduced to such a fortune as she has lived upon these late years, and that she should lose that which she brought, as well as that which was her husband's. Yet, I hear, she has now got some of her own land in Ireland granted her; but whether she will get it when she comes there is, I think, a question.

We have a lady new come into this country that I pity, too, extremely. She is one of my Lord of Valentia's daughters,* and has married an old fellow that is some threescore and ten, who has a house that is fitter for the hogs than for her, and a fortune that will not at all recompense the least of these inconveniences. Ah! 'tis most certain I should have chosen a handsome chain to lead my apes in before such a husband; but marrying and hanging go by destiny, they say. It was not mine, it seems, to have an emperor; the spiteful man, merely to vex me, has gone and married my countrywoman, my Lord Lee's daughter.† What a multitude of willow garlands‡ shall I wear before I die; I think I had best make them into faggots this cold weather, the flame they would make in a chimney would be of more use to me than that which was in the hearts of all those that gave them me, and would last as long. I did not think I should have got thus far. I have been so persecuted with visits all this week§ I have had no time to despatch anything of business, so that now I have done this I have forty letters more to write; how much rather would I have them all to you than to anybody else; or, rather, how much better would it be if there needed none to you, and that I could tell you without writing how much I am

Yours.

* The daughters of Viscount Valentia, who lived near Newport Pagnell when not in Ireland.
† Sir Justinian Isham had just married the daughter of Lord Leigh of Stoneleigh, Warwickshire. Dorothy calls her countrywoman because the lady had lived at one time at Leighton Buzzard.
‡ Traditionally given to forsaken lovers.
§ Probably visits of condolence on the death of Robin Osborne.

Letter 38

Dorothy gives Temple an account of a sermon she has heard. She asks him to address his letters differently in future. She mentions the news that Cromwell's nominated Parliament has voted for the abolition of the Court of Chancery.

[SEPTEMBER 1653]

SIR, If want of kindness were the only crime I exempted from pardon, 'twas not that I had the least apprehension you could be guilty of it; but to show you (by excepting only an impossible thing) that I excepted nothing. No, in earnest, I can fancy no such thing of you, or if I could, the quarrel would be to myself; I should never forgive my own folly that led me to choose a friend that could be false. But I'll leave this (which is not much to the purpose) and tell you how, with my usual impatience, I expected your letter, and how cold it went to my heart to see it so short a one. 'Twas so great a pain to me that I am resolv'd you shall not feel it; nor can I in justice punish you for a fault unwillingly committed. If I were your enemy, I could not use you ill when I saw Fortune do it too, and in gallantry and good nature both, I should think myself rather obliged to protect you from her injuries (if it lay in my power) than double them upon you. These things considered, I believe this letter will be longer than ordinary—kinder I think it cannot be. I always speak my heart to you; and that is so much your friend, it never furnishes me with anything to your disadvantage. I am glad you are an admirer of Telesile★ as well as I; in my opinion 'tis a fine Lady, but I know you will pity poor Amestris★ strangely when you have read her story. I'll swear I cried for her when I read it first, though she were but an imaginary person; and, sure, if anything of that kind can deserve it, her misfortunes may.

God forgive me, I was as near laughing yesterday where I should not. Would you believe that I had the grace to go hear a sermon upon a week day? In earnest, 'tis true; and Mr. Marshall†

★ Characters in *Le Grand Cyrus*.

† Stephen Marshall, a famous divine and supporter of the Puritan cause.

103

was the man that preached, but never anybody was so defeated.* He is so famed that I expected rare things of him, and seriously I listened to him at first with as much reverence and attention as if he had been St. Paul; and what do you think he told us? Why, that if there were no kings, no queens, no lords, no ladies, nor gentlemen, nor gentlewomen, in the world, 'twould be no loss at all to God Almighty. This we had over some forty times, which made me remember it whether I would or not. The rest was much at this rate, interlarded with the prettiest odd phrases, that I had the most ado to look soberly enough for the place I was in that ever I had in my life. He does not preach so always, sure? If he does, I cannot believe his sermons will do much towards the bringing anybody to heaven more than by exercising their patience. Yet, I'll say that for him, he stood stoutly for tithes,† though, in my opinion, few deserved them less than he; and it may be he would be better without them.

Yet you are not convinced, you say, that to be miserable is the way to be good; to some natures I think it is not, but there are many of so careless and vain a temper, that the least breath of good fortune swells them with so much pride, that if they were not put in mind sometimes by a sound cross or two that they are mortal, they would hardly think it possible; and though 'tis a sign of a servile nature when fear produces more of reverence in us than love, yet there is more danger of forgetting oneself in a prosperous fortune than in the contrary, and affliction may be the surest (though not the pleasantest) guide to heaven. What think you, might not I preach with Mr. Marshall for a wager? But you could fancy a perfect happiness here, you say; that is not much, many people do so; but I never heard of anybody that had it more than in fancy, so that 'twill not be strange if you should miss on't. One may be happy to a good degree, I think, in a faithful friend, a moderate fortune, and a retired life; further than this I know nothing to wish; but if there be anything beyond it, I wish it you.

You did not tell me what carried you out of town in such

* Disappointed.

† Cromwell's nominated assembly was at that time considering the question of abolishing the tithe system.

haste. I hope the occasion was good, you must account to me for all that I lost by it. I shall expect a whole packet next week. Oh, me! I have forgot this once or twice to tell you, that if it be no inconvenience to you, I could wish you would change the place of direction for my letters. Certainly that Jones knows my name, I bespoke a saddle of him once, and though it be a good while agone, yet I was so often with him about it—having much ado to make him understand how I would have it, it being of a fashion he had never seen, though since it be common—that I am confident he has not forgot me. Besides that, upon it he got my brother's custom; and I cannot tell whether he does not use the shop still. Jane presents her humble service to you, and has sent you something in a box; 'tis hard to imagine what she can find here to present you withal, and I am much in doubt whether you will not pay too dear for it if you discharge the carriage. 'Tis a pretty freedom she takes, but you may thank your-self; she thinks because you call her fellow-servant, she may use you accordingly. I bred her better, but you have spoiled her.

Is it true that my Lord Whitelocke goes Ambassador where my Lord Lisle should have gone? I know not how he may appear in a Swedish Court, but he was never meant for a courtier at home, I believe. Yet 'tis a gracious Prince; he is often in this country, and always does us the favour to send his fruit hither. He was making a purchase of one of the best houses in the county. I know not whether he goes on with it; but 'tis such a one as will not become anything less than a lord. And there is a talk as if the Chancery were going down;* if so, his title goes with it, I think. 'Twill be sad news for my Lord Keble's son,† he will have nothing left to say when 'my Lord, my father,' is taken from him. Were it better that I had nothing to say neither, than that I should entertain you with such senseless things. I hope I am half asleep, nothing else can excuse me; if I were quite

---

* On August 5th the nominated Parliament had voted for the abolition of the Court of Chancery.

† Richard Keble was a judge and one of the three Commissioners for the custody of the Great Seal. His son was Joseph Keble, who had anything but a distinguished career.

asleep, I should say fine things to you; I often dream I do; but perhaps if I could remember them they are no wiser than my waking discourses. Good-night.

Letter 39

One of Dorothy's letters to Temple has gone astray, and she asks him to investigate the matter. She chides him for having caught a cold.

[SEPTEMBER 1653]

SIR, That you may be at more certainty hereafter what to think, let me tell you that nothing could hinder me from writing to you (as well for my own satisfaction as yours) but an impossibility of doing it; nothing but death or a dead palsy in my hands, or something that had the same effects. I did write, and gave it Harrold, but by an accident his horse fell lame, so that he could not set out on Monday; but a Tuesday he did come to town; on Wednesday, carried the letter himself (as he tells me) where 'twas directed, which was to Mr. Copyn in Fleet Street. 'Twas the first time I made use of that direction; no matter and I had not done it then, since it proves no better. Harrold came late home on Thursday night with such an account as your boy gave you: that coming out of town the same day he came in, he had been at Fleet Street again, but there was no letter for him. I was sorry, but I did not much wonder at it because he gave so little time, and resolved to make my best of that I had by Collins. I read it over often enough to make it equal with the longest letter that ever was writ, and pleased myself, in earnest (as much as it was possible for me in the humour I was in), to think how by that time you had asked me pardon for the little reproaches you had made me, and that the kindness and length of my letter had made you amends for the trouble it had given you in expecting it. But I am not a little amazed to find you had it not. I am very confident it was delivered, and therefore you must search where the fault lies.

Were it not that you have suffered too much already, I would complain a little of you. Why should you think me so careless of anything that you were concerned in, as to doubt that I had not writ? Though I had received none from you, I should not have taken that occasion to revenge myself. Nay, I should have concluded you innocent, and have imagined a thousand ways how it might happen, rather than have suspected your want of kindness. Why should not you be as just to me? But I will not chide, it may be (as long as we have been friends) you do not know me so well yet as to make an absolute judgment of me; but if I know myself at all, if I am capable of being anything, 'tis a perfect friend. Yet I must chide too. Why did you get such a cold? Good God! how careless you are of a life that (by your own confession) I have told you makes all the happiness of mine. 'Tis unkindly done. What is left for me to say, when that will not prevail with you; or how can you persuade me to a care of myself, when you refuse to give me the example? I know nothing in the world that gives me the least desire of preserving myself, but the opinion I have you would not be willing to lose me; and yet, if you saw with what caution I live (at least to what I did before), you would reproach it to yourself sometimes, and might grant, perhaps, that you have not got the advantage of me in friendship so much as you imagine. What (besides your consideration) could oblige me to live and lose all the rest of my friends thus one after another? Sure I am not insensible nor very ill-natured, and yet I'll swear I think I do not afflict myself half so much as another would do that had my losses. I pay nothing of sadness to the memory of my poor brother, but I presently disperse it with thinking what I owe in thankfulness that 'tis not you I mourn for.

Well, give me no more occasions to complain of you, you know not what may follow. Here was Mr. Freeman* yesterday that made me a very kind visit, and said so many fine things to me, that I was confounded with his civilities, and had nothing to say for myself. I could have wished then that he had considered me less and my niece more; but if you continue to use me thus, in

* See Letters 26 and 27. Freeman had told Temple on one occasion that he had been deterred from paying suit to Dorothy because of her stately bearing.

earnest, I'll not be so much her friend hereafter. Methinks I see you laugh at all my threatenings; and not without reason. Mr. Freeman, you believe, is designed for somebody that deserves him better. I think so too, and am not sorry for it; and you have reason to believe I never can be other than your faithful friend.

Letter 40

Dorothy gives her views on style in letter-writing, and goes on to discuss the translation of French romances. She encloses a letter she has had from her brother-in-law, Sir Thomas Peyton.

[SEPTEMBER 1653]

SIR, Pray, let not the apprehension that others say finer things to me make your letters at all the shorter; for, if it were so, I should not think they did, and so long you are safe. My brother Peyton does, indeed, sometimes send me letters that may be excellent for aught I know, and the more likely because I do not understand them; but I may say to you (as to a friend) I do not like them, and have wondered that my sister (who, I may tell you too, and you will not think it vanity in me, had a great deal of wit, and was thought to write as well as most women in England) never persuaded him to alter his style, and make it a little more intelligible. He is an honest gentleman, in earnest, has understanding enough, and was an excellent husband to two very different wives, as two good ones could be. My sister was a melancholy, retired woman, and, besides the company of her husband and her books, never sought any, but could have spent a life much longer than hers was in looking to her house and her children. This lady is of a free, jolly humour, loves cards and company, and is never more pleased than when she sees a great many others that are so too. Now, with both these he so perfectly complied that 'tis hard to guess which humour he is more inclined to in himself; perhaps to neither, which makes it so much the more strange. His kindness to his first wife may give him an esteem for her sister; but he was too much smitten with this lady to think of marrying anybody else, and, seriously, I could not blame him, for she had, and has yet, great loveliness in her; she was very handsome, and is very good (one may read it in her face at first sight); a woman that is hugely civil to all people, and takes as generally as anybody that I know, but not more than my cousin Molle's letters do, which, yet, you do not like, you say, nor I neither, I'll swear; and if it be ignorance in us both we'll forgive it one another. In my opinion these great scholars are not the best writers (of letters, I mean); of books, perhaps they are. I never had, I think, but one letter from Sir Justinian, but 'twas worth twenty of anybody's else to make me sport. It was the most sublime nonsense that in my life I ever read; and yet, I believe, he descended as low as he could to come near my weak understanding. 'Twill be no compliment after this to say I like your letters in themselves; not as they come from one that is not indifferent to me, but, seriously, I do. All letters, methinks, should be free and easy as one's discourse; not studied as an oration, nor made up of hard words like a charm. 'Tis an admirable thing to see how some people will labour to find out terms that may obscure a plain sense. Like a gentleman I knew, who would never say 'the weather grew cold,' but that 'winter began to salute us'. I have no patience for such coxcombs, and cannot blame an old uncle of mine that threw the standish at his man's head because he writ a letter for him where, instead of saying (as his master bid him), 'that he would have writ himself, but that he had the gout in his hand;' he said 'that the gout in his hand would not permit him to put pen to paper.' The fellow thought that he had mended it mightily, and that putting pen to paper was much better than plain writing.

I have no patience neither for these translators of romances. I met with *Polexander* and *L'illustre Bassa*★ both so disguised that I, who am their old acquaintance, hardly knew them; besides that, they were still so much French in words and phrases that 'twas impossible for one that understood not French to make anything of them. If poor *Prazimene*★ be in the same dress, I

★ *Polexandre,* by Marin le Roy de Gomberville, 1632; an English translation appeared in 1647. *Ibrahim ou l'illustre Bassa* was by the same writer as *Le Grand Cyrus,* M. de Scudéry. *La Prazimène,* by Le Maire, Paris, 1643. See note † on p. 110

would not see her for the world. She has suffered enough besides. I never saw but four tomes of her, and was told the gentleman that writ her story died when those were finished. I was very sorry for it, I remember, for I liked so far as I had seen of it extremely. Is it not my good Lord of Monmouth,* or some such honourable personage, that presents her to the English ladies? I have heard many people wonder how he spends his estate. I believe he undoes himself with printing his translations. Nobody else will undergo the charge, because they never hope to sell enough of them to pay themselves withal. I was looking t'other day in a book of his where he translates *Pipeur* 'a piper,' and twenty words more that are as false as this.

My Lord Broghill† sure, will give us something worth the reading. My Lord Saye,‡ I am told, has writ a romance since his retirement in the Isle of Lundy, and Mr. Waller,§ they say, is making one of our wars, which, if he does not mingle with a great deal of pleasing fiction, cannot be very diverting, sure, the subject is so sad.

But all this is nothing to my coming to town, you'll say. 'Tis confest; and that I was willing as long as I could to avoid saying anything when I had nothing to say worth your knowing. I am still obliged to wait my brother Peyton and his lady's coming. I had a letter from him this week, which I will send you, that you may see what hopes he gives. As little room as I have left, too, I must tell you what a present I had made me to-day. Two of the finest young Irish greyhounds that ere I saw; a gentleman that serves the General sent them me. They are newly come over, and sent for by Henry Cromwell, he tells me, but not how he got them for me. However, I am glad I have them, and much the more because it dispenses with a very unfit employment that

* Henry Carey, Earl of Monmouth. He had started to publish translations of romances in 1637.

† Roger Boyle, Lord Broghill, third son of the Earl of Cork. After the Restoration he had a new title, Earl of Orrery. He was later a friend of Dryden, Davenant, and Cowley. A translation of *La Prazimène*, by 'R.B.', was extant in 1707. This was undoubtedly Boyle's work.

‡ No trace of this romance is to be found.

§ The poet and politician. Nothing is known of a romance by him.

your father, out of his kindness to you and his civility to me, was content to take upon him.

Good Sister

I am very sorry to hear of the loss of our good brother, whose short time gives us a sad example of our frail condition. But I will say the less, knowing whom I write to, whose religion and wisdom is a present stay and support in all worldly accidents.

'Tis long since we resolved to have given you a visit, and have relieved you of my daughter. But I have had the following of a most laborious affair, which hath cost me the travelling, though in our own country still, fifty miles a week; and have been less at home than elsewhere ever since I came from London; which hath vext me the more in regard I have been detained from the desire I had of being with you before this time. Such entertainment, however, must all those have that have to do with such a purse-strong and wilful person as Sir Edward Hales. This next week being Michaelmas week, we shall end all and I be at liberty, I hope, to consider my own contentments. In the meantime I know not what excuses to make for the trouble I have put you to already, of which I grow to be ashamed, and should much more be so if I did not know you to be as good as you are fair. In both which regards I have a great honour to be esteemed,

My good sister,
Your faithful brother
And servant,
Thomas Peyton.

Knowlton, Sept. 22nd, 1653.

ON THE OTHER SIDE OF SIR T. PEYTON'S LETTER

Nothing that is paper can 'scape me when I have time to write, and 'tis to you. But that I am not willing to excite your envy, I would tell you how many letters I have despatched since I ended yours; and if I could show them you 'twould be a certain cure for it, for they are all very short ones, and most of them merely compliments, which I am sure you care not for.

I had forgot in my other to tell you what Jane requires for the satisfaction of what you confess you owe her. You must promise her to be merry, and not to take cold when you are at the tennis court, for there she hears you are found.

Because you mention my Lord Broghill and his wit, I have sent you some of his verses.* My brother urged them against me

* These verses and the love-letter mentioned later have not survived.

one day in a dispute, where he would needs make me confess that no passion could be long lived, and that such as were most in love forgot that ever they had been so within a twelvemonth after they were married; and, in earnest, the want of examples to bring for the contrary puzzled me a little, so that I was fain to bring out these pitiful verses of my Lord Biron to his wife, which was so poor an argument that I was e'en ashamed on't myself, and he quickly laughed me out of countenance with saying they were just such as a married man's flame would produce and a wife inspire. I send you a love letter, too; which, simple as you see, it was sent me in very good earnest, and to a person of quality, as I was told. If you read it when you go to bed, 'twill certainly make you sleep approved.

I am yours.

Letter 41

Dorothy dines with a rich widow, and argues the advantages of wealth with her brother Henry. She tells Temple of her father's poor state of health.

[OCTOBER 1653]

SIR, The day I should have received your letter I was invited to dine at a rich widow's* (whom I think I once told you of, and offered my service in case you thought fit to make addresses there); and she was so kind, and in so good humour, that if I had had any commission I should have thought it a very fit time to speak. We had a huge dinner, though the company was only of her own kindred that are in the house with her and what I brought; but she is broke loose from an old miserable husband that lived so long, she thinks if she does not make haste she shall not have time to spend what he left. She is old and was never handsome, and yet is courted a thousand times more than the greatest beauty in the world would be that had not a fortune. We could not eat in quiet for the letters and presents that came in from people that would not have looked upon her when they

* Lady Briers of Upbury, Pulloxhill.

had met her if she had been left poor. I could not but laugh to myself at the meanness of their humour, and was merry enough all day, for the company was very good; and besides I expected to find when I came home a letter from you that would be more a feast and company to me than all that was there. But never anybody was so defeated* as I was to find none. I could not imagine the reason, only I assured myself it was no fault of yours, but perhaps a just punishment upon me for having been too much pleased in a company where you were not.

After supper my brother and I fell into dispute about riches, and the great advantages of it; he instanced in the widow that it made one respected in the world. I said 'twas true, but that was a respect I should not at all value when I owed it only to my fortune. And we debated it so long till we had both talked ourselves weary enough to go to bed. Yet I did not sleep so well but that I chid my maid for waking me in the morning, till she stopped my mouth with saying she had letters for me. I had not patience to stay till I could rise, but made her tie up all the curtains to let in light; and amongst some others I quickly found my dear letter that was first to be read, and which made all the rest not worth the reading. I could not but wonder to find in it that my cousin Franklin† should want a true friend when 'tis thought she has the best husband in the world; he was so passionate for her before he had her, and so pleased with her since, that, in earnest, I did not think it possible she could have anything left to wish for that she had not already in such a husband with such a fortune. But she can best tell whether she is happy or not; only if she be not, I do not see how anybody else can hope for it. I know her the least of all the sisters, and perhaps 'tis to my advantage that she knows me no more, since she speaks so obligingly of me.‡ But do you think it was altogether without

* Disappointed.
† Elizabeth, wife of Richard Franklin of Moor Park, Herts., sister of Tom Cheke, and youngest daughter of Sir Thomas Cheke, whose first wife was Dorothy's aunt. Franklin had purchased Moor Park in May 1652.
‡ At this time the friendship between Temple and the Franklins was new. It must have grown later, since he and Dorothy were to spend their honeymoon there.

design that she spoke it to you? When I remember she is Tom Cheke's sister, I am apt to think she might have heard his news, and meant to try whether there was anything of truth in't. My cousin Molle, I think, means to end the summer there. They say, indeed, 'tis a very fine seat, but if I did not mistake Sir Thomas Cheke, he told me there was never a good room in the house. I was wondering how you came by an acquaintance there, because I had never heard you speak that you knew them. I never saw him in my life, but he is famous for a kind husband. Only 'twas found fault with that he could not forbear kissing his wife before company, a foolish trick that young married men, it seems, are apt to; he has left it long since, I suppose. But, seriously, 'tis as ill a sight as one would wish to see, and appears very rude, methinks, to the company.

What a strange fellow this goldsmith is, he has a head fit for nothing but horns. I chid him once for a seal he set me just of this fashion and the same colours; and if he were to make twenty they should be all so, his invention can stretch no further than blue and red. It makes me think of the fellow that could paint nothing but a flower-de-luce, who, when he met with one that was so firmly resolved to have a lion for his sign that there was no persuading him on't, 'Well,' says the painter, 'let it be a lion then, but it shall be as like a flower-de-luce* as e'er you saw.' So, because you would have it a dolphin, he consented to it, but it is liker an ill-favoured knot of ribbon. I did not say anything of my father's being ill of late; I think I told you before, he kept his chamber ever since his last sickness, and so he does still. Yet I cannot say that he is at all sick, but has so general a weakness upon him that I am much afraid their opinion of him has too much of truth in't, and do extremely apprehend how the winter may work upon him. Will you pardon this strange scribbled letter, and the disorderliness on't? I know you would, though I should not tell you that I am not so much at leisure as I used to be. You can forgive your friends anything, and when I am not the faithfulest of those, never forgive me. You may direct your letter how you please, here will be nobody to receive it but

Yours.

* Fleur-de-lis.

Letter 42

Temple has given Dorothy some advice as to how to refute her brother's arguments concerning him and their friendship. She goes on to give her views on thoughtless marriages, and to discuss the various rumours that have been circulating about herself and Temple; she says she will never deny them if asked, but would be happier if no one knew.

[OCTOBER 1653]

SIR, You have furnished me now with arguments to convince my brother, if he should ever enter upon the dispute again. In earnest, I believed all this before, but 'twas something an ignorant* kind of faith in me. I was satisfied myself, but could not tell how to persuade another of the truth on't; and to speak indifferently, there are such multitudes that abuse the names of love and friendship, and so very few that either understand or practise it in reality, that it may raise great doubts whether there is any such thing in the world or not, and such as do not find it in themselves will hardly believe 'tis anywhere. But it will easily be granted, that most people make haste to be miserable; that they put on their fetters as inconsiderately as a woodcock runs into a noose, and are carried by the weakest considerations imaginable to do a thing of the greatest consequence of anything that concerns this world. I was told by one (who pretends to know him very well) that nothing tempted my cousin Osborne to marry his lady (so much) as that she was an Earl's daughter;† which methought was the prettiest fancy, and had the least of sense in it, of any I had heard on, considering that it was no addition to her person, that he had honour enough before for his fortune, and how little 'tis esteemed in this age—if it be anything in a better—which for my part I am not well satisfied in. Beside that, in this particular it does not sound handsomely. My Lady Bridget Osborne makes a worse name a great deal, methinks, than plain my Lady Osborne would do.

* Somewhat ignorant.
† Dorothy's cousin, Sir Thomas Osborne, had recently married Lady Bridget Bertie, daughter of the Earl of Lindsey.

And now I speak of cousins let me tell you that (allowing all that Mrs. Franklin* said of the person she recommended to you to be but compliment, or that she thought she could not say less upon such an occasion) I may confess I think she meant me and spoke it as you say *malicieusement*. For 'tis true her husband was proposed by one that is our neighbour and has some interest in the family as a trustee for the estate I think. I heard my mother speak of it once, for how it fell to the ground I cannot tell. Perhaps he was a little engaged then where he is now fast.

I have been studying how Tom Cheke† might come by his intelligence, and I verily believe he has it from my cousin Peters. She lives near them in Essex, and in all likelihood, for want of other discourse to entertain him withal, she has come out with all she knows. The last time I saw her she asked me for you before she had spoke six words to me; and I, who of all things do not love to make secrets of trifles, told her I had seen you that day. She said no more, nor I neither; but perhaps it worked in her little brain. The best on't is, the matter is not great, for though I confess I had rather nobody knew it, yet 'tis that I shall never be ashamed to own.

How kindly do I take these civilities of your father's; in earnest, you cannot imagine how his letter pleased me. I used to respect him merely as he was your father, but I begin now to owe it to himself; all that he says is so kind and so obliging, so natural and so easy, that one may see 'tis perfectly his disposition, and has nothing of disguise in it. 'Tis long since that I knew how well he writes, perhaps you have forgot that you showed me a letter of his (to a French Marquis, I think, or some such man of his acquaintance) when I first knew you; I remember it very well, and that I thought it as handsome a letter as I had seen; but I have not skill it seems, for I like yours too.

You shall excuse me for giving you leave to believe that I might have been happy if I could have resolved to have been so

* Dorothy is referring to Temple's conversation with Mrs Franklin, mentioned in Letter 41.

† Dorothy refers to the suspicion she has that Cheke was one of the people responsible for spreading rumours about her attachment to Temple. See Letters 27 and 41.

116

without you. 'Tis very true that I never tried to resolve it, for if I had I think it had been to very little purpose. But if I could have done that I know not whether I should have been e'er a whit the nearer being happy. If one could be so for resolving it t'were not so hard a thing to get as 'tis believed.

Is not your cousin Rant* left a rich widow? I was told so to-day, and that she is very handsome too. A fine house I am sure she has, it was my Lord Paget's. That name makes me remember to tell you that I had a letter t'other day from my Lady,† where she sends me the news of her sister Isabella's being come over. If you saw it you would conclude with me that where she loves 'tis with passion. She is as absolutely wild with joy as anything in Bedlam is mad, and all that she says is so strangely disjointed that one who did not know her would think she were a very odd body. But yet it is a thousand times more natural than the Oxford letter you sent me.‡ I do not envy that kind of wit by no means; such extravagances as you say seldom mean anything.

I can pardon all my cousin Franklin's little plots of discovery, if she believed herself when she said she was confident our humours would agree extremely well. In earnest, I think they do; for I mark that I am always of your opinion, unless it be when you will not allow that you write well, for there I am too much concerned. Jane told me t'other day very soberly that we writ very much alike. I think she said it with an intent to please me, and did not fail in't; but if you write ill, 'twas no great compliment to me. *A propos de* Jane, she bids me tell you that, if you liked your marmalade of quince,§ she could send you more and she thinks better, that has been made since.

'Twas a strange caprice, as you say, of Mrs. Harrison, but there is fate as well as love in those things. The Queen took the greatest pains to persuade her from it that could be; and (as

* Jane Rant, Temple's first cousin, whose husband had just died. Their home was in Norwich.

† Lady Diana Rich's elder sister Frances was married to Lord Paget.

‡ In Letter 40 Dorothy had said 'these great scholars are not the best writers (of letters, I mean)'. Temple has obviously sent her a letter from some Oxford scholar, illustrating his comments on what she said.

§ This tells us what was in the parcel Jane Wright sent to Temple, mentioned in Letter 38.

somebody says, I know not who) 'Majesty is no ill orator;' but all would not do. When she had nothing to say for herself she told her she had rather beg with Mr. Howard than live in the greatest plenty that could be with either my Lord Broghill, Charles Rich, or Mr. Nevile—for all these were dying for her then. I am afraid she has altered her opinion since 'twas too late, for I do not take Mr. Howard to be a person that can deserve one should neglect all the world for him. And where there is no reason to uphold a passion, it will sink of itself; but where there is, it may last

Eternally, I am yours.

Letter 43

Dorothy has no news about a trip to London; she must wait until her brother-in-law comes for his daughter. She refers to her argument with her brother about marrying for advantage and not for love, and mentions more examples of unsuitable matches. She tells Temple he must be careful of his health for her sake.

[OCTOBER 1653]

SIR, You would have me say something of my coming. Alas! how fain I would have something to say, but I know no more than you saw in that letter I sent you.* How willingly would I tell you anything that I thought would please you; but I confess I do not love to give uncertain hopes, because I do not care to receive them. And I thought there was no need of saying I would be sure to take the first occasion, and that I waited with impatience for it, because I hoped you had believed all that already; and so you do, I am sure. Say what you will, you cannot but know my heart enough to be assured that I wish myself with you, for my own sake as well as yours. 'Tis rather that you love to hear me say it often, than that you doubt it; for I am no dissembler. I could not cry for a husband that were indifferent to me (like your cousin);† no, nor for a husband that I loved neither.

* Thomas Peyton's letter enclosed in Letter 40.
† Mrs Rant of Norwich. See Letter 42.

I think 'twould break my heart sooner than make me shed a tear. 'Tis ordinary griefs that only make me weep. In earnest, you cannot imagine how often I have been told that I had too much *franchise*★ in my humour, and that 'twas a point of good breeding to disguise handsomely; but I answered still for myself, that 'twas not to be expected I should be exactly bred, that had never seen a Court since I was capable of anything. Yet I know so much—that my Lady Carlisle† would take it very ill if you should not let her get the point of honour; 'tis all she aims at, to go beyond everybody in compliment. But are not you afraid of giving me a strange vanity with telling me that I write better than the most extraordinary person in the kingdom? If I had not the sense to understand that the reason why you like my letters better is only because they are kinder than hers, such a word might have undone me.

But my Lady Isabella,‡ that speaks, and looks, and sings, and plays, and all so prettily, why cannot I say that she is as free from faults as her sister believes her? No; I am afraid she is not, and sorry that those she has are so generally known. My brother did not bring them for an example,§ but I did, and made him confess she had better have married a beggar than that beast with all his estate. She cannot be excused; but certainly they run a strange hazard that have such husbands as makes them think they cannot be more undone, whatever course they take. Oh, 'tis ten thousand pities! I remember she was the first woman that ever I took notice of for extremely handsome; and, in earnest, she was then the loveliest thing that could be looked on, I think. But what should she do with beauty now? Were I as she, I would hide myself from all the world; I should think all people that looked

★ Frankness, openness, freedom of speech.

† Lucy, Countess of Carlisle was the daughter of the Earl of Northumberland and sister of the Countess of Leicester mentioned later in this letter. Her great beauty and wit inspired poets like Carew, Cartwright, Davenant, and Waller. She was involved in much intrigue connected with the court and was a prisoner in the Tower between 1649 and 1652.

‡ Sister of Lady Diana Rich and wife of Sir James Thynne.

§ In the argument mentioned in Letter 41. Dorothy and Henry had been arguing about the importance of riches and 'advantage' in marriage, as opposed to love.

on me read it in my face and despised me in their hearts; and at the same time they made me a leg, or spoke civilly to me, I should believe they did not think I deserved their respect. I'll tell you who he urged for an example though, my Lord Pembroke and my Lady, who, they say, are upon parting after all his passion for her, and his marrying her against the consent of all his friends; but to that I answered, that though he pretended great kindness he had for her, I never heard of much she had for him, and knew she married him merely for advantage. Nor is she a woman of that discretion as to do all that might become her, when she must do it rather as things fit to be done than as things she is inclined to. Besides that, what with a *spleenatick* side and a *chimickall* head, he is but an odd body himself.

But is it possible what they say, that my Lord Leicester and my Lady are in great disorder, and that after forty years' patience he has now taken up the cudgels and resolves to venture for the mastery? Methinks he wakes out of his long sleep like a froward child, that wrangles and fights with all that comes near it. They say he has turned away almost every servant in the house, and left her at Penshurst to digest it as she can.

What an age do we live in, where 'tis a miracle if in ten couple that are married, two of them live so as not to publish to the world that they cannot agree. I begin to be of the opinion of him that (when the Roman Church first propounded whether it were not convenient for priests not to marry) said that it might be convenient enough, but sure it was not our Saviour's intention, for He commanded that all should take up their cross and follow Him; and for his part, he was confident there was no such cross as a wife. This is an ill doctrine for me to preach; but to my friends I cannot but confess that I am afraid much of the fault lies in us; for I have observed that generally in great families, the men seldom disagree, but the women are always scolding; and 'tis most certain, that let the husband be what he will, if the wife have but patience (which, sure, becomes her best), the disorder cannot be great enough to make a noise; his anger alone, when it meets with nothing that resists it, cannot be loud enough to disturb the neighbours. And such a wife may be said to do as a kinswoman of ours that had a husband who was not always himself; and when he was otherwise, his humour was to rise in the night, and with two bedstaves tabour upon the table an hour together. She took care every night to lay a great cushion upon the table for him to strike on, that nobody might hear him, and so discover his madness. But 'tis a sad thing when all one's happiness is only that the world does not know you are miserable.

For my part, I think it were very convenient that all such as intend to marry should live together in the same house some years of probation; and if, in all that time, they never disagreed, they should then be permitted to marry if they pleased; but how few would do it then! I do not remember that I ever saw or heard of any couple that were bred up so together (as many you know are, that are designed for one another from children), but they always disliked one another extremely; and parted, if it were left in their choice. If people proceeded with this caution, the world would end sooner than is expected, I believe; and because, with all my wariness, 'tis not impossible but I may be caught, nor likely that I should be wiser than everybody else, 'twere best, I think, that I said no more in this point.

What would I give to know that sister of yours that is so good at discovery; sure she is excellent company; she had reason to laugh at you when you would have persuaded her the 'moss was sweet.' I remember Jane brought some of it to me, to ask me if I thought it had no ill smell, and whether she might venture to put it in the box or not. I told her as I thought, she could not put a more innocent thing there, for I did not find that it had any smell at all; besides that I was willing it should do me some service in requital of the pains I had taken for it. My niece and I wandered through some six hundred acres of wood in search of it, to make rocks and strange things that her head is full of, and she admires it more than you did. If she had known I had consented it should have been used to fill up a box, she would have condemned me extremely. I told Jane that you liked her present, and she, I find, is resolved to spoil your compliment, and make you confess at last that they are not worth the eating; she threatens to send you more, but you would forgive her if you saw how she baits me every day to go to London; all that I can say will not satisfy her. When I urge (as 'tis true) that there is a necessity of my stay here, she grows furious, cries you will die with melancholy, and confounds me so with stories of your ill-humour, that I'll swear I think I should go merely to be at quiet, if it were possible, though there were no other reason for it. But I hope 'tis not so ill as she would have me believe it, though I know your humour is strangely altered from what it was, and am sorry to see it. Melancholy must needs do you more hurt than to another to whom it may be natural, as I think it is to me; therefore if you loved me you would take heed on't. Can you believe that you are dearer to me than the whole world besides, and yet neglect yourself? If you do not, you wrong a perfect friendship; and if you do, you must consider my interest in you, and preserve yourself to make me happy. Promise me this, or I shall haunt you worse than she does me. Scribble how you please, so you make your letter long enough; you see I give you good example; besides, I can assure you we do perfectly agree if you receive no satisfaction but from my letters, I have none but what yours give me.

Letter 44

Dorothy tells Temple he must take care of his health. She outlines her ideas of the conditions for a happy marriage and the qualities she would want to find in a husband.

[OCTOBER 1653]

SIR, Why are you so sullen, and why am I the cause? Can you believe that I do willingly defer my journey? I know you do not. Why, then, should my absence now be less supportable to you than heretofore? It cannot, nay it shall not be long (if I can help it), and I shall break through all inconveniences rather than deny you anything that lies in my power to grant. But by your own rules, then, may not I expect the same from you? Is it possible that all I have said cannot oblige you to a care of yourself? What a pleasant distinction you make when you say 'tis not melancholy makes you do these things, but a careless forgetfulness. Did ever anybody forget themselves to that degree that was not melancholy in extremity? Good God! how are you altered; and what is it that has done it? I have known you when of all the things in the world you would not have been taken for a discontent; you were, as I thought, perfectly pleased with your condition; what has made it so much worse since? I know nothing you have lost, and am sure you have gained a friend. A friend that is capable of the highest degree of friendship you can propound, that has already given an entire heart for that which she received, and 'tis no more in her will than in her power ever to recall it or divide it; if this be not enough to satisfy you, tell me what I can do more? I shall find less difficulty in the doing it than in imagining what it may be; and will not you then do so much for my sake as to be careful of a health I am so infinitely concerned in and which those courses must needs destroy? If you loved me you would I am sure you would, and let me tell you, you can never be that perfect friend you describe if you can deny me this. But will not your wife* believe there is such a friendship? I am not of her opinion at all, but I do not wonder neither that she is of it. Alas! how few there are that ever heard of such a thing, and fewer that understand it. Besides it is not to be taught or learned. It must come naturally to those that have it, and those must believe it before they can know it. But I admire, since she has it not, how she can be satisfied of her condition; nothing else, sure, can recompense the alterations you say it made in her fortune. What was it took her? Her husband's good face? What could invite her where there was neither fortune, wit, nor good usage, and a husband to whom she was but indifferent; which is all one to me, if not worse than an aversion, and I should sooner hope to gain upon one that hated me than upon one that did not consider me enough either to love or hate me. I'll swear she is a great deal easier to please than I should be.

There are a great many ingredients must go to the making me happy in a husband. First, as my cousin Franklin says, our humours must agree; and to do that he must have that kind of

* There is no reference that tells us who the person was that Temple had mentioned in the letter to which this is the answer.

123

breeding that I have had, and used that kind of company. That is, he must not be so much a country gentleman as to understand nothing but hawks and dogs, and be fonder of either than of his wife; nor of the next sort of them whose aim reaches no further than to be Justice of Peace, and once in his life High Sheriff, who reads no books but statutes, and studies nothing but how to make a speech interlarded with Latin that may amaze his disagreeing poor neighbours, and fright them rather than persuade them into quietness. He must not be a thing that began the world in a free school, was sent from thence to the university, and is at his furthest when he reaches the Inns of Court, has no acquaintance but those of his form in these places, speaks the French he has picked out of old laws, and admires nothing but the stories he has heard of the revels that were kept there before his time. He must not be a town gallant neither, that lives in a tavern and an ordinary, that cannot imagine how an hour should be spent without company unless it be in sleeping, that makes court to all the women he sees, thinks they believe him, and laughs and is laughed at equally. Nor a travelled Monsieur whose head is all feather inside and outside, that can talk of nothing but dances and duels, and has courage enough to wear slashes when everybody else dies with cold to see him. He must not be a fool of no sort, nor peevish, nor ill-natured, nor proud, nor covetous; and to all this must be added, that he must love me and I him as much as we are capable of loving. Without all this, his fortune, though never so great, would not satisfy me; and with it, a very moderate one would keep me from ever repenting my disposal.

I have been as large and as particular in my descriptions as my cousin Molle in his of Moor Park—but that you know the place so well I would send it you—nothing can come near his patience in writing it, but my reading on't. But would you had sent me your father's letter, it would not have been less welcome to me than to you; and you may safely believe that I am equally concerned with you in anything. I should be pleased, too, to see something of my Lady Carlisle's writing, because she is so extra-ordinary a person. I have been thinking of sending you my picture till I could come myself; but a picture is but dull company, and that you need not; besides, I cannot tell whether it be very like me or not, though 'tis the best I ever had drawn for me, and Mr. Lely will have it that he never took more pains to make a good one in his life, and that was it I think that spoiled it. He was condemned for making the first he drew for me a little worse than I, and in making this better he has made it as unlike as t'other. He is now, I think, at my Lord Paget's at Marlow, where I am promised he shall draw a picture of my Lady for me—she gives it me, she says, as the greatest testimony of her friendship to me, for by her own rule she is past the time of having pictures taken of her. After eighteen, she says, there is no face but decays apparently; I would fain have had her excepted such as had never been beauties, for my comfort, but she would not.

When you see your friend Mr. Heningham, you may tell him in his ear there is a willow garland coming towards him.* He might have sped better in his suit if he had made court to me, as well as to my Lady Ruthin. She has been my wife† this seven year, and whosoever pretends there must ask my leave. I have now given my consent that she shall marry a very pretty little gentleman, Sir Christopher Yelverton's son, and I think we shall have a wedding ere it be long. My Lady her mother, in great kindness, would have recommended Heningham to me, and told me in a compliment that I was fitter for him than her daughter, who was younger, and therefore did not understand the world so well; that she was certain if he knew me he would be extremely taken for I would make just that kind of wife he looked for. I humbly thanked her, but said that without knowing him more than by relation, I was certain he would not make that kind of husband I looked for—and so it went no further.

I expect my elder brother here shortly, whose fortune is well mended by my other brother's death, so as if he were satisfied

---

* Mr Heningham seems to have been an unsuccessful suitor in other directions, too: apart from Lady Ruthin, he is mentioned in Letter 64 as having been jilted by a Miss Gerard. The willow garland was traditionally presented to the forsaken lover.

† An expression not uncommon in letters of the period. A form of address (and compliment) between great women friends: one would refer to the other as 'wife', and the compliment would be reciprocated by the use of 'husband'.

himself with what he has done,* I know no reason why he might not be very happy; but I am afraid he is not. I have not seen my sister† since I knew she was so; but, sure, she can have lost no beauty, for I never saw any that she had, but good black eyes, which cannot alter. He loves her, I think, at the ordinary rate of husbands, but not enough, I believe, to marry her so much to his disadvantage if it were to do again; and that would kill me were I as she, for I could be infinitely better satisfied with a husband that had never loved me in hope he might, than with one that began to love me less than he had done.

I am yours.

Letter 45

Dorothy is still worried about the delay in her proposed visit to London and the disappointment this is causing Temple. She has sent Temple her portrait in miniature and apologizes for not sending the original. Temple has said that in her last letter she told him what qualities she would not want in a husband, but she supposed that he would know what kind of husband she would have.

[SUNDAY OCTOBER THE 23RD, 1653]

SIR, You say I abuse you; and Jane says you abuse me when you say you are not melancholy. Which is to be believed? Neither, I think; for I could not have said so positively (as it seems she did) that I should not be in town till my brother came back: he was not gone when she writ, nor is not yet; and if my brother Peyton had come before his going, I had spoiled her prediction. But now it cannot be; for he goes on Monday or Tuesday at farthest. I hope you deal truly with me, too, in saying that you are not melancholy (though she does not believe it). I am thought so, many times, when I am not at all guilty on't. How often do I sit in company a whole day, and when they are gone am not able to give an account of six words that was said, and many times

---

* John Osborne had recently married, and we can suppose that the marriage was not altogether a good one.

† John Osborne's new wife, Eleanor Danvers.

could be so much better pleased with the entertainment my own thoughts give me, that 'tis all I can do to be so civil as not to let them see they trouble me. This may be your disease. However, remember you have promised me to be careful of yourself, and that if I secure what you have entrusted me with, you will answer for the rest. Be this our bargain then; and look that you give me as good an account of one as I shall give you of t'other. In earnest, I was strangely vexed to see myself forced to disappoint you so, and felt your trouble and my own too. How often have I wished myself with you, though but for a day, for an hour: I would have given all the time I am to spend here for it with all my heart.

You could not have but laughed if you had seen me last night. My brother and Mr. Gibson were talking by the fire; and I sat by, but as no part of the company. Amongst other things (which I did not at all mind), they fell into a discourse of flying; and both agreed that it was very possible to find out a way that people might fly like birds, and despatch their journeys so: I, that had not said a word all night, started up at that, and desired they would say a little more in it, for I had not marked the beginning; but instead of that, they both fell into so violent a laughing, that I should appear so much concerned in such an art; but they little knew of what use it might have been to me. Yet I saw you last night, but 'twas in a dream; and before I could say a word to you, or you to me, the disorder* my joy to see you had put me into waked me. Just now I was interrupted, too, and called away to entertain two dumb gentlemen;—you may imagine whether I was pleased to leave my writing to you for their company;—they have made such a tedious visit, too; and I am so tired with making of signs and tokens for everything I had to say. Good God! how do those that live always with them? They are brothers; and the eldest is a baronet, has a good estate, a wife and three or four children. He was my servant heretofore, and comes to see me still for old love's sake; but if he could have made me mistress of the world I could not have had him; and yet I'll swear he has nothing to be disliked in him but his want of tongue, which in a woman might have been a virtue.

* Mental disturbance, upset, excitement.

I sent you a part of *Cyrus* last week, where you will meet with one Doralize in the story of Abradate and Panthée. The whole story is very good; but her humour makes the best part of it. I am of her opinion in most things that she says in her character of '*L'honnest homme*' that she is in search of, and her resolution of receiving no heart that had been offered to anybody else. Pray, tell me how you like her, and what fault you find in my Lady Carlisle's letter?* Methinks the hand and the style both show her a great person, and 'tis writ in the way that's now affected by all that pretend to wit and good breeding; only, I am a little scandalised I confess that she uses that word faithful—she that never knew how to be so in her life.

I have sent you my picture because you wished for it; but, pray, let it not presume to disturb my Lady Sunderland's. Put it in some corner where no eyes may find it out but yours, to whom it is only intended. 'Tis no very good one, but the best I shall ever have drawn of me; for, as my Lady says, my time for pictures is past, and therefore I have always refused to part with this, because I was sure the next would be a worse. There is a beauty in youth that everybody had once in their lives; and I remember my mother used to say there was never anybody (that was not deformed) but were handsome, to some reasonable degree, once between fourteen and twenty. It must hang with the light on the left of it; and you may keep it if you please till I bring you the original. But then I must borrow it (for 'tis no more mine, if you like it), because my brother is often bringing people into my closet where it hangs, to show them other pictures that are there; and if he should miss this long from thence, 'twould trouble his jealous head.

You are not the first that has told me I knew better what qualities I would not have in a husband than what I would; but it was more pardonable in them. I thought you had understood better what kind of person I liked than anybody else could possibly have done, and therefore did not think it necessary to make you that description too. Those that I reckoned up were only such as I could not be persuaded to have upon no terms,

* In Letter 44 Dorothy had expressed a wish to see an example of Lady Carlisle's art as a letter writer, and Temple has obviously sent her one.

though I had never seen such a person in my life as Mr. Temple; not but that all those may make very good husbands to some women; but they are so different from my humour that 'tis not possible we should ever agree; for though it might be reasonably enough expected that I should conform mine to theirs (to my shame be it spoken), I could never do it. And I have lived so long in the world, and so much at my own liberty, that whosoever has me must be content to take me as they find me, without hope of ever making me other than I am. I cannot so much as disguise my humour. When it was designed that I should have had Sir Jus., my brother used to tell me he was confident that, with all his wisdom, any woman that had wit and discretion might make an ass of him, and govern him as she pleased. I could not deny but possibly it might be so, but 'twas that I was sure I could never do; and though 'tis likely I should have forced my-self to so much compliance as was necessary for a reasonable wife, yet farther than that no design could ever have carried me; and I could not have flattered him into a belief that I admired him, to gain more than he and all his generation are worth.

'Tis such an ease (as you say) not to be solicitous to please others: in earnest, I am no more concerned whether people think me handsome or ill-favoured, whether they think I have wit or that I have none, than I am whether they think my name Elizabeth or Dorothy. I would do nobody no injury; but I should never desire to please above one; and that one I must love too, or else I should think it a trouble, and consequently not do it. I have made a general confession to you; will you give me absolution? Methinks you should; or you are not much better by your own relation; therefore 'tis easiest for us to forgive one another. When you hear anything from your father, remember that I am his humble servant, and much concerned in his good health.

I am yours.

Dorothy and Temple were not to be separated for much longer: the anxiously awaited visit of Sir Thomas Peyton and his wife to Chicksands to fetch their daughter (she had been with Dorothy all the summer) took place at last. In his diary, Henry Osborne says that they arrived on October 25th, and that on October 28th he and Dorothy accompanied the

Peytons to London. Dorothy stayed in London until November 25th, and must have seen Temple whenever possible. But the visit was also a great strain on them both: the attitude of her brother Henry towards the affair had so far been frustrating but bearable, as the tone of Dorothy's letters to Temple throughout the summer of 1653 shows; now, with her every movement under her brother's surveillance, this attitude made the chances of their ever reaching a satisfactory outcome seem hopeless. It is not surprising that they appear to have been on edge and unable to give themselves completely to the happiness of reunion. Among the undated notes written by Dorothy there are some that reflect this situation, and show the beginnings of the period of hopelessness and depression recorded in the letters written from Chicksands after Dorothy's return home. It is difficult to place these notes among those written during Dorothy's earlier visit to London in February 1653, and during her later visit from April to June the following year, when Temple was in Ireland. References to her cousin Mrs Franklin and to visits to the home of the Countess of Devonshire at Roehampton also speak in favour of November 1653 as the correct date for the following notes:

I

I find my conscience a little troubled till I have asked your pardon for my ill humour last night, will you forgive it me? In earnest, I could not help it, but I met with a cure for it: my brother kept me up to hear his lecture till after two o'clock and I spent all my ill humour upon him, and yet we parted very quietly and looked as if a little good fortune might make us good friends. But your special friend my eldest brother, I have a story to tell you of him; will my cousin Franklin come, think you? Send me word, it may be 'twas but a compliment. If I can see you this morning I will, but I dare not promise it.

II

Now I have got the trick of breaking my word I shall do it every day. I must go to Roehampton today, but 'tis all one, you do not care much for seeing me. Well, my master, remember last night you swaggered like a young lord, I'll make your stomach come down; rise quickly you had best and come hither that I may give you your lesson this morning before I go.

III

I have slept as little as you and may be allowed to talk as unreasonably. Yet I find I am not quite senseless, I have a heart still that cannot resolve to refuse you anything within its power to grant. But Lord! where shall I see you? People will think me mad if I go abroad this morning after having seen me in the condition I was in last night, and they will think it strange to see you here. Could you not stay till they are all gone to Roehampton? They go this morning. I do but ask though, do what you please, only believe you do a great injustice if you think me false. I never resolved to give you an eternal farewell, but I resolved at the same time to part with all the comfort of my life and, whether I told it you or not, I shall die

Yours.

Tell me what you will have me do.

IV

Here comes the note again to tell you I cannot call on you tonight; I cannot help it and you must take it as patiently as you can, but I am engaged tonight at the Three Kings to sup and play. Poor man, I am sorry for you in earnest. I shall be quite spoiled, I see no remedy; think whether it were not best to leave me and begin a new adventure.

After her return to Chicksands at the end of November, Dorothy's letters reflect a mood of deepening despair and depression. This can be ascribed to a variety of causes, chief of which was undoubtedly the strain on her nerves during the short reunion with Temple, and the apparent hopelessness of their mutual future. But there were other circumstances: she no longer had the cheering company of her young niece, and her companion Jane Wright was ill; her father's health was rapidly deteriorating, and the gossip about Temple and herself increased, resulting in renewed attempts by her brother to find a husband for her elsewhere.

Letter 46

Dorothy has returned to Chicksands and is looking ill.

[SATURDAY NOVEMBER THE 26TH, 1653]

Had you the bit of paper I sent you from St. Albans? 'Twas a strange one I believe, as my humour was when I writ it. Well here I am, God knows for how long or how short a time, nor shall I be able to guess till all our company that we expect is come; then as I find their humours I shall resolve. Why did not you tell me how ill I looked? All people here will not believe but I have been desperately sick. I do not find I am ill though, but I have lost a collop* that's certain, and now I am come to my own glass I find I have not brought down the same face I carried up. But 'tis no matter, 'tis well enough for this place.

I shall hear from you a Thursday, and next week I shall be able to say much more than I can this, both because I shall have more time, and besides I shall know more. You will send the picture and forget not that you must walk no more in the cloisters. No, in earnest, 'tis not good for you, and you must be ruled by me in that point. Besides if we do not take care of ourselves I find nobody else will. I would not live, though, if I had not some hope left that a little time may breathe great alterations, and that 'tis possible we may see an end of our misfortune. When that hope leaves us then 'tis time to die, and if I know myself I should need no more to kill me. Let your letter be as much too long as this is too short, I shall find by that how I must write. I do not think this is sense, nor have I time to look it over.

I am yours.

Henry Osborne's diary tells us that he discussed Dorothy and Temple with his brother-in-law, Sir Thomas Peyton, on the day she left London. He then returned to Chicksands, and on the following day, November 29th, made the following entry: 'My sister resolved not to marry Temple.'

There is possibly a letter missing here, or perhaps Dorothy spent a very miserable week deciding what to say to Temple.

Letter 47

Dorothy tells Temple that the only way to put an end to their misfortunes is to separate, and to admit that the future holds nothing for them.

* She has lost a lot of weight.

SIR, Having tired myself with thinking, I mean to weary you with reading, and revenge myself that way for all the unquiet thoughts you have given me. But I intended this a sober letter, and therefore, *sans raillerie*, let me tell you, I have seriously considered all our misfortunes, and can see no end of them but by submitting to that which we cannot avoid, and by yielding to it break the force of a blow which if resisted brings a certain ruin. I think I need not tell you how dear you have been to me, nor that in your kindness I placed all the satisfaction of my life; 'twas the only happiness I proposed to myself, and had set my heart so much upon it that it was therefore made my punishment, to let me see that, how innocent soever I thought my affection, it was guilty in being greater than is allowable for things of this world. 'Tis not a melancholy humour gives me these apprehensions and inclinations, nor the persuasions of others; 'tis the result of a long strife with myself, before my reason could overcome my passion, or bring me to a perfect resignation to whatsoever is allotted for me. 'Tis now done, I hope, and I have nothing left but to persuade you to that, which I assure myself your own judgment will approve in the end, and your reason has often prevailed with you to offer; that which you would have done then out of kindness to me and point of humour,* I would have you do now out of wisdom and kindness to yourself. Not that I would disclaim my part in it or lessen my obligation to you, no, I am your friend as much as ever I was in my life, I think more, and am sure I shall never be less. I have known you long enough to discern that you have all the qualities that make an excellent friend, and I shall endeavour to deserve that you may be so to me; but I would have you do this upon the justest grounds, and such as may conduce most to your quiet and future satisfaction. When we have tried all ways to happiness, there is no such thing to be found but in a mind conformed to one's condition, whatsoever it be, and in not aiming at anything that is either impossible or improbable; all the

---

* In Letter 19 Temple had said that he would release her from her promises if she wished.

rest is but vanity and vexation of spirit, and I durst pronounce it so from that little knowledge I have had of the world, though I had not Scripture for my warrant. The shepherd that bragged to the traveller, who asked him, 'What weather it was like to be?' that it should be what weather pleased him, and made it good by saying it should be what weather pleased God, and what pleased God should please him, said an excellent thing in rude language, and knew enough to make him the happiest person in the world if he made a right use on't. There can be no pleasure in a struggling life, and that folly which we condemn in an ambitious man, that's ever labouring for that which is hardly got and more uncertainly kept, is seen in all according to their several humours; in some 'tis covetousness, in others pride, in some a stubbornness of nature that chooses to go always against the tide, and in others an unfortunate fancy to things that are in themselves innocent till we make them otherwise by desiring them too much. Of this sort I think you, and I, are; we have lived hitherto upon hopes so airy that I have often wondered how they could support the weight of our misfortunes; but passion gives a strength above nature, we see it in mad people; and, not to flatter ourselves, ours is but a refined degree of madness. What can it be else to be lost to all things in the world but that single object that takes up one's fancy, to lose all the quiet and repose of one's life in hunting after it, when there is so little likelihood of ever gaining it, and so many more probable accidents that will infallibly make us miss of it? And, which is more than all, 'tis being mastered by that which reason and religion teaches us to govern, and in that only gives us a pre-eminence above beasts. This, soberly consider'd, is enough to let us see our error, and consequently to persuade us to redeem it. To another person, I should justify myself that 'tis not a lightness in my nature, nor any interest that is not common to us both, that has wrought this change in me. To you that know my heart, and from whom I shall never hide it, to whom a thousand testimonies of my kindness can witness the reality of it, and whose friendship is not built upon common grounds, I have no more to say but that I impose not my opinions upon you, and that I had rather you took them up as your own choice than upon my entreaty. But if, as we have not differed in anything else, we could agree in this too, and resolve upon a friendship that will be much the perfecter for having nothing of passion in it, how happy might we be without so much as a fear of the change that any accident could bring. We might defy all that fortune could do, and putting off all disguise and constraint, with that which only made it necessary, make our lives as easy to us as the condition of this world will permit. I may own you as a person that I extremely value and esteem, and for whom I have a particular friendship, and you may consider me as one that will always be

Your faithful.

This was writ when I expected a letter from you, how came I to miss it? I thought at first it might be the carrier's fault in changing his inn without giving notice, but he assures me he did, to Nan. My brother's groom came down to-day, too, and saw her, he tells me, but brings me nothing from her; if nothing of ill be the cause, I am contented. You hear the noise my Lady Anne Blunt* has made with her marrying? I am so weary with meeting it in all places where I go. From what is she fallen! they talked but the week before that she should have my Lord of Strafford.† Did you not intend to write to me when you writ to Jane? That bit of paper did me great service; without it I should have had strange apprehension, all my sad dreams, and the several frights I have waked in, would have run so in my head that I should have concluded something of very ill from your silence. Poor Jane is sick, but she will write, she says, if she can. Did you send the last part of *Cyrus* to Mr. Hollingsworth?

* A topical scandal. Anne Blunt (or Blount), daughter of the Earl of Newport, was accused of breach of promise. She denied having contracted marriage, and later petitioned the Protector to be cleared of the calumny; this petition was undoubtedly the expression of her father's attitude to what had been, to use Dorothy's words in Letter 48, a 'senseless passion'. (Dorothy seems to suggest that she was already married, but this was not the case.)

† The son of the Strafford executed in 1641.

Letter 48

Dorothy tells Temple that nothing he can say will make her change her resolve to bring their relationship to an end. She is determined to replace passion with friendship, and implores him to try to do likewise.

[FRIDAY DECEMBER THE 16TH, 1653]

SIR, I am extremely sorry that your letter miscarried, but I am confident my brother has it not. As cunning as he is, he could not hide it so from me, but that I should discover it some way or other. No; he was here, and both his men, when this letter should have come, and not one of them stirred out that day; indeed, the next they went all to London. The note you writ to Jane came in one of Nan's, by Collins, but nothing else; it must be lost by the porter that was sent with it, and 'twas very unhappy that there should be anything in it of more consequence than ordinary; it may be numbered amongst the rest of our misfortunes, all which an inconsiderate passion has occasioned. You must pardon me I cannot be reconciled to it, it has been the ruin of us both. 'Tis true that nobody must imagine to themselves ever to be absolute masters on't, but there is great difference betwixt that and yielding to it, between striving with it and soothing it up till it grows too strong for one. Can I remember how ignorantly and innocently I suffered it to steal upon me by degrees; how under a mask of friendship I cozened myself into that which, had it appeared to me at first in its true shape, I had feared and shunned? Can I discern that it has made the trouble of your life, and cast a cloud upon mine, that will help to cover me in my grave? Can I know that it wrought so upon us both as to make neither of us friends to one another, but agree in running widly to our own destructions, and that perhaps of some innocent persons* who might live to curse our folly that gave them so miserable a being? Ah! if you love yourself or me, you must confess that I have reason to condemn this senseless passion; that wheresoe'er it comes destroys all that entertain it; nothing of judgment or discretion can live with it, and puts everything else

* The children that they might have in the future.

out of order before it can find a place for itself. What has it not brought my poor Lady Anne Blunt to? She is the talk of all the footmen and boys in the street, and will be company for them shortly, who yet is so blinded by her passion as not at all to perceive the misery she has brought herself to; and this fond love of hers has so rooted all sense of nature out of her heart, that, they say, she is no more moved than a statue with the affliction of a father and mother that doted on her, and had placed the comfort of their lives in her preferment. With all this is it not manifest to the whole world that Mr. Blunt could not consider anything in this action but his own interest, and that he makes her a very ill return for all her kindness; if he had loved her truly he would have died rather than have been the occasion of this misfortune to her. My cousin Franklin* (as you observe very well) may say fine things now she is warm in Moor Park, but she is very much altered in her opinions since her marriage, if these be her own. She left a gentleman, that I could name, whom she had much more of kindness for than ever she had for Mr. Franklin, because his estate was less; and upon the discovery of some letters that her mother intercepted, suffered herself to be persuaded that twenty-three hundred pound a year was better than twelve, though with a person she loved; and has recovered it so well, that you see she confesses there is nothing in her condition she desires to alter at the charge of a wish. She's happier by much than I shall ever be, but I do not envy her; may she long enjoy it, and I an early and a quiet grave, free from the trouble of this busy world, where all with passion pursue their own interests at their neighbour's charges; where nobody is pleased but somebody complains on't; and where 'tis impossible to be without giving and receiving injuries.

You would know what I would be at, and how I intend to dispose of myself. Alas! were I in my own disposal, you should come to my grave to be resolved; but grief alone will not kill. All that I can say, then, is that I resolve on nothing but to arm myself with patience, to resist nothing that is laid upon me, nor struggle for what I have no hope to get. I have no ends nor no

* Mrs Franklin had probably tried to persuade Temple to ignore the dictates of prudence and marry for the sake of his passion.

137

designs, nor will my heart ever be capable of any; but like a country wasted by a civil war, where two opposing parties have disputed their right so long till they have made it worth neither of their conquests, 'tis ruined and desolated by the long strife within it to that degree as 'twill be useful to none—nobody that knows the condition 'tis in will think it worth the gaining, and I shall not cozen anybody with it. No, really, if I may be permitted to desire anything, it shall be only that I may injure nobody but myself—I can bear anything that reflects only upon me; or, if I cannot, I can die; but I would fain die innocent, that I might hope to be happy in the next world, though never in this. I take it a little ill that you should conjure me by anything, with a belief that 'tis more powerful with me than your kindness. No, assure yourself what that alone cannot gain will be denied to all the world. You would see me, you say? You may do so if you please, though I know not to what end. You deceive yourself if you think it would prevail upon me to alter my intentions; besides, I can make no contrivances; it must be here, and I must endure the noise it will make, and undergo the censures of a people that choose ever to give the worst interpretation that anything will bear. Yet if it can be any ease to you to make me more miserable than I am, never spare me; consider yourself only, and not me at all—'tis no more than I deserve for not accepting what you offered me whilst 'twas in your power to make it good, as you say it then was. You were prepared, it seems, but I was surprised, I confess it. 'Twas a kind fault though; and you may pardon it with more reason than I have to forgive it myself. And let me tell you this, too, as lost and as wretched as I am, I have still some sense of my reputation left in me—I find that to my last—I shall attempt to preserve it as clear as I can; and to do that I must, if you see me thus, make it the last of our interviews. What can excuse me if I should entertain any person that is known to pretend to me, when I can have no hope of ever marrying him? And what hope can I have of that when the fortune that can only make it possible to me depends upon a thousand accidents and contingencies, the uncertainty of the place 'tis in, and the government it may fall under, your father's life or his success, his disposal of himself and then of his fortune, besides the time that must necessarily be required to produce all this, and the changes that may probably bring with it, which 'tis impossible for us to foresee? All this considered, what have I to say for myself when people shall ask, what 'tis I expect? Can there be anything vainer than such a hope upon such grounds? You must needs see the folly on't yourself, and therefore examine your own heart what 'tis fit for me to do, and what you can do for a person you love, and that deserves your compassion if nothing else—a person that will always have an inviolable friendship for you, a friendship that shall take up all the room my passion held in my heart, and govern there as master, till death come to take possession and turn it out.

Why should you make an impossibility where there is none? A thousand accidents might have taken me from you, and you must have borne it. Why should not your own resolution work as much upon you as necessity and time does infallibly upon all people? Your father would take it very ill, I believe, if you should pretend to love me better than he did my Lady, yet she is dead and he lives, and perhaps may do to love again. There is a gentle-woman in this country that loved so passionately for six or seven years that her friends, who kept her from marrying, fearing her death, consented to it; and within half a year her husband died, which afflicted her so strangely nobody thought she would have lived. She saw no light but candles in three years, nor came abroad in five; and now that 'tis some nine years past, she is passionately taken again with another, and how long she has been so nobody knows but herself. This is to let you see 'tis not impossible what I ask, nor unreasonable. Think on't, and attempt it at least; but do it sincerely, and do not help your passion to master you. As you have ever loved me do this.

The carrier shall bring your letter to Suffolk House to Jones. I shall long to hear from you; but if you should deny me the only hope that's left me, I must beg you will defer it till Christmas Day be past; for, to deal freely with you, I have some devotions to per-form then, which must not be disturbed with anything, and nothing is like to do it as so sensible an affliction.

Adieu.

Letter 49

Temple has accused her of being false and inconstant, and has said that he hopes she can find a prince who will marry her. Dorothy says she has nothing more to do in the world except leave it.

[SATURDAY DECEMBER THE 24TH, 1653]

SIR, 'Tis most true what you say, that few have what they merit; if it were otherwise, you would be happy, I think, but then I should be so too, and that must not be—a false and an inconstant person cannot merit it, I am sure. You are kind in your good wishes, but I aim at no friends nor no princes, the honour would be lost upon me; I should become a crown so ill, there would be no striving for it after me, and, sure, I should not wear it long. Your letter was a much greater loss to me than that of Henry Cromwell* and, therefore, 'tis that with all my care and diligence I cannot inquire it out. You will not complain, I believe, of the shortness of my last, whatsoever else you dislike in it, and if I spare you at any time 'tis because I cannot but imagine, since I am so wearisome to myself, that I must needs be so to everybody else, though, at present, I have other occasions† that will not permit this to be a long one. I am sorry it should be only in my power to make a friend miserable, and that where I have so great kindness I should do so great injuries; but 'tis my fortune, and I must bear it; 'twill be none to you, I hope, to pray for you, nor to desire that you would (all passion laid aside) freely tell me my faults, that I may, at least, ask your forgiveness where 'tis not in my power to make you better satisfaction. I would fain make even with all the world, and be out of danger of dying in anybody's debt; then I have nothing more to do in it but to expect when I shall be so happy as to leave it, and always to remember that my

* Son of the Protector. Temple had probably referred to the opportunity she had had at one time of marrying Cromwell; by this time Cromwell was married to someone else.

† We learn from Henry Osborne's diary that during the Christmas period he and Dorothy had an exhausting round of social duties to perform and entertained a great deal themselves.

misfortune makes all my fault towards you, and that my faults to God made all my misfortunes.

Your unhappy.

Letter 50

Dorothy says she can pity the unhappiness she has caused Temple, but she cannot love him. She feels no concern even for her nearest relations. She begs him to take any course that will make him happy. She signs the letter 'your humble servant', a form she has not used since Letter 14.

[SATURDAY DECEMBER THE 31ST, 1653]

SIR, I can say little more than I did—I am convinced of the vileness of the world and all that's in 't, and that I deceived myself extremely when I expected anything of comfort from it. No, I have no more to do in it but to grow every day more and more weary of it, if it be possible that I have not yet reached the highest degree of hatred for it. But I thank God I hate nothing else but the bare world, and the vices that make a part of it. I am in perfect charity with my enemies, and have compassion for all people's misfortunes as well as for my own, especially for those I may have caused; and I may truly say I bear my share of such. But as nothing obliges me to relieve a person that is in extreme want till I change conditions with him and come to be where he began, and that I may be thought compassionate enough if I do all that I can without prejudicing my self too much, so let me tell you, that if I could help it, I would not love you, and that as long as I live I shall strive against it as against that which has been my ruin, and was certainly sent me as a punishment for my sins. But I shall always have a sense of your misfortunes, equal, if not above, my own. I shall pray that you may obtain a quiet I never hope for but in my grave, and I shall never change my condition but with my life. Yet let this not give you a hope. Nothing can ever persuade me to enter the world again. I shall, in a short time, have disengaged myself of all my little affairs in it, and settled myself in a condition to apprehend nothing but too long a life, therefore I wish you would forget me; and to induce you to it, let me tell you freely that I deserve you should. If I remember anybody, 'tis against my will. I am possessed with that strange insensibility that my nearest relations have no tie upon me, and I find myself no more concerned in those that I have heretofore had great tenderness of affection for, than in my kindred that died long before I was born. Leave me to this, and seek a better fortune. I beg it of you as heartily as I forgive you all those strange thoughts you have had of me. Think me so still if that will do anything towards it. For God sake do take any course that may make you happy; or, if that cannot be, less unfortunate at least than

Your friend and humble servant,
D. OSBORNE.

I can hear nothing of that letter, but I hear from all the people that I know, part of my unhappy story, and from some that I do not know. A lady, whose face I never saw, sent it me as news she had out of Ireland.

Letter 51

Dorothy tells Temple to preserve himself from the violence of his passions by venting them on her. She asks for his forgiveness.

[SATURDAY JANUARY THE 7TH, 1654]

If you have ever loved me, do not refuse the last request I shall ever make you; 'tis to preserve yourself from the violence of your passion. Vent it all upon me; call me and think me what you please; make me, if it be possible, more wretched than I am. I'll bear it all without the least murmur. Nay, I deserve it all, for had you never seen me you had certainly been happy. 'Tis my misfortunes only that have that infectious quality as to strike at the same time me and all that's dear to me. I am the most unfortunate woman breathing, but I was never false. No; I call heaven to witness that if my life could satisfy for the least injury my fortune has done you (I cannot say 'twas I that did them you), I would lay it down with greater joy than any person ever received a crown; and if I ever forget what I owe you, or ever entertain a thought of kindness for any person in the world besides, may I live a long and miserable life. 'Tis the greatest curse I can invent; if there be a greater, may I feel it. This is all I can say. Tell me if it be possible I can do anything for you, and tell me how I may deserve your pardon for all the trouble I have given you. I would not die without it.

FOR MR. TEMPLE.

Letter 52

She is worried lest her last letter has been misunderstood. She says she would do anything to restore his peace of mind, but cannot give him any hope of a resumption of their former relationship. Why cannot he control his passion? She is anxious about the desperate things he has said. They must submit to God's decree.

[SATURDAY JANUARY THE 7TH, 1654]

SIR, That which I writ by your boy was in so much haste and distraction as I cannot be satisfied with it, nor believe it has expressed my thoughts as I meant them. No, I find it is not easily done at more leisure, and I am yet to seek what to say that is not too little nor too much. I would fain let you see that I am extremely sensible of your affliction, that I would lay down my life to redeem you from it, but that's a mean expression; my life is of so little value that I will not mention it. No, let it be rather what, in earnest, if I can tell anything I have left that is considerable enough to expose for it, it must be that small reputation I have amongst my friends, that's all my wealth, and that I could part with to restore you to that quiet you lived in when I first knew you. But, on the other side, I would not give you hopes of that I cannot do. If I loved you less I would allow you to be the same person to me, and I would be the same to you as heretofore. But to deal freely with you, that were to betray myself, and I find that my passion would quickly be my master again if I gave it any liberty. I am not secure that it would not make me do the most extravagant things in the world, and I shall be forced to keep a continual war alive with it as long as there are any remainders of it left;—I think I might as well have said as long as I lived. Why should you give yourself over so unreasonably to it? Good God! no woman breathing can deserve half the trouble you give yourself. If I were yours from this minute I could not recompense what you have suffered from the violence of your passion, though I were all that you can imagine me, when, God knows, I am an inconsiderable person, born to a thousand misfortunes, which have taken away all sense of anything else from me, and left me a walking misery only. I do from my soul forgive you all the injuries your passion has done me, though, let me tell you, I was much more at my ease whilst I was angry. Scorn and despite would have cured me in some reasonable time, which I despair of now. However, I am not displeased with it, and, if I may be of any advantage to you, I shall not consider myself in it; but let me beg, then, that you will leave off those dismal thoughts. I tremble at the desperate things you say in your letter; for the love of God, consider seriously with yourself what can enter into comparison with the safety of your soul. Are a thousand women, or ten thousand worlds, worth it? No, you cannot have so little reason left as you pretend, nor so little religion. For God sake let us not neglect what can only make us happy for a trifle. If God had seen it fit to have satisfied our desires we should have had them, and everything would not have conspired thus to cross them. Since He has decreed it otherwise (at least as far as we are able to judge by events), we must submit, and not by striving make an innocent passion a sin, and show a childish stubbornness.

I could say a thousand things more to this purpose if I were not in haste to send this away, that it may come to you, at least, as soon as the other.

Adieu.

I cannot imagine who this should be that Mr. Dr.* meant, and am inclined to believe 'twas a story made to disturb you, though perhaps not by him.

FOR MR. T.

* Unidentified. Mentioned in Letters 54 and 60. Apparently Temple had been told a malicious story about Dorothy having greeted a Mr Dr in St Gregory's Church during her stay in London. Temple's jealousy contributed to Dorothy's depression on her return to Chicksands.

Letter 53

Since she cannot cure him of his passion, she confesses that she never really had any hope of conquering her own. He still has the same place in her heart, and she says she will marry him if fortune allows.

[SUNDAY JANUARY THE 8TH, 1654]

SIR, 'Tis never my humour to do injuries, nor was this* meant as any to you. No, in earnest, if I could have persuaded you to have quitted a passion that injures you, I had done an act of real friendship, and you might have lived to thank me for it; but since it cannot be, I will attempt it no more. I have laid before you the inconveniences it brings along, how certain the trouble is, and how uncertain the reward; how many accidents may hinder us from ever being happy, and how few there are (and those so unlikely) to make up our desires. All this makes no impression in you; you are still resolved to follow your blind guide, and I to pity where I cannot help. It will not be amiss though to let you see that what I did was merely in consideration of your interest, and not at all of my own, that you may judge of me accordingly; and, to do that, I must tell you that, unless it were after the receipt of those letters that made me angry, I never had the least hope of wearing out my passion, nor, to say truth, much desire. For to what purpose should I have strived against it? 'Twas innocent enough in me that resolved never to marry, and would have kept me company in this solitary place as long as I lived, without being a trouble to myself or anybody else. Nay, in earnest, if I could have hoped that you would be so much your own friend as to seek out a happiness in some other person, nothing under heaven could have satisfied me like entertaining myself with the thought of having done you service in diverting you from a troublesome pursuit of what is so uncertain, and by that giving you the occasion of a better fortune. Otherwise, whether you loved me still, or whether you did not, was equally the same to me, your interest set aside. I will not reproach you how ill an interpretation you made of this, because we'll have no

* Her desire to end their attachment.

more quarrels. On the contrary, because I see 'tis in vain to think of curing you, I'll study only to give you what ease I can, and leave the rest to better physicians—to time and fortune. Here, then, I declare that you have still the same power in my heart that I gave you at our last parting*, that I will never marry any other; and that if ever our fortunes will allow us to marry, you shall dispose me as you please; but this, to deal freely with you, I do not hope for. No; 'tis too great a happiness, and I, that know myself best, must acknowledge I deserve crosses and afflictions, but can never merit such a blessing. You know 'tis not a fear of want that frights me. I thank God I never distrusted His providence, nor I hope never shall, and without attributing anything to myself, I may acknowledge He has given me a mind that can be satisfied within as narrow a compass as that of any person living of my rank. But I confess that I have an humour will not suffer me to expose myself to people's scorn. The name of love is grown so contemptible by the folly of such as have falsely pretended to it, and so many giddy people have married upon that score and repented so shamefully afterwards, that nobody can do anything that tends towards it without being esteemed a ridiculous person. Now, as my young Lady Holland† says, I never pretended to wit in my life, but I cannot be satisfied that the world should think me a fool, so that all I can do for you will be to preserve a constant kindness for you, which nothing shall ever alter or diminish; I'll never give you any more alarms, by going about to persuade you against that you have for me; but from this hour we'll live quietly, no more fears, no more jealousies; the wealth of the whole world, by the grace of God, shall not tempt me to break my word with you, nor the importunity of all the friends I have. Keep this as a testimony against me if ever I do, and make me a reproach to them by it; therefore be secure, and rest satisfied with what I can do for you.

You should come hither but that I expect my brother every day; not but that he designed a longer stay when he went, but since he keeps his horses with him 'tis an infallible token that he

* Apparently their parting when Dorothy left London at the end of November had been a perfectly affectionate one.
  † Elizabeth, wife of Lord Holland, Lady Diana Rich's brother.

is coming. We cannot miss fitter times than this, twenty in a year, and I shall be as ready to give you notice of such as you can be to desire it, only you would do me a great pleasure if you could forbear writing, unless it were sometimes on great occasions. This is a strange request for me to make, that have been fonder of your letters than my Lady Protector is of her new honour,* and, in earnest, could be so still but there are a thousand inconveniences in't that I could tell you. Tell me what you can do; in the meantime think of some employment for yourself this summer. Who knows what a year may produce? If nothing, we are but where we were, and nothing can hinder us from being, at least, perfect friends. Adieu. There's nothing so terrible in my other letter but you may venture to read it. Have not you forgot my Lady's book?

Temple's very natural reaction to these last letters was to insist on coming to see Dorothy. He visited Chicksands on the 12th or 13th of January. Whatever passed between them, it is clear that Temple left her, happy in the knowledge that he had succeeded in dispelling her fears and anxieties. They were now more firmly committed to one another than they had ever been. Henry Osborne was not told of this; they deliberately misled him, as the entry in his diary for January 13th shows: 'I came to Chicksands before dinner. I found Mr. Temple here, and my sister broke with him, God be praised.'

Letter 54

Dorothy asks Temple whether they will be forgiven for lying to her brother. She was overjoyed to see him again, and hopes that they will both have patience to wait for what the future may bring.

[FRIDAY—SUNDAY JANUARY THE 13TH—15TH, 1654]

'Tis but an hour since you went, and I am writing to you already; is not this kind? How do you after your journey; are you not weary; do you not repent that you took it to so little purpose? Well, God forgive me, and you too, you made me tell a great lie.

* Cromwell had accepted the title of Lord Protector on December 15th, 1653.

I was fain to say you came only to take your leave before you went abroad; and all this not only to keep quiet,* but to keep him from playing the madman; for when he has the least suspicion, he carries it so strangely that all the world takes notice on't, and so often guess at the reason, or else he tells it. Now, do but you judge whether if by mischance he should discover the truth, whether he would not rail most sweetly at me (and with some reason) for abusing† him. Yet you helped to do it; a sadness that he discovered at your going away inclined him to believe you were ill satisfied, and made him credit what I said. He is kind now in extremity, and I would be glad to keep him so till a discovery is absolutely necessary. Your going abroad will confirm him much in his belief, and I shall have nothing to torment me in this place but my own doubts and fears. Here I shall find all the repose I am capable of, and nothing will disturb my prayers and wishes for your happiness which only can make mine. Your journey cannot be to your disadvantage neither; you must needs be pleased to visit a place‡ you are so much concerned in, and to be a witness yourself of the probability of your hopes, though I will believe you need no other inducement to this voyage than my desiring it. I know you love me, and you have no reason to doubt my kindness. Let us both have patience to wait what time and fortune will do for us; they cannot hinder our being perfect friends.

Lord, there were a thousand things I remembered after you were gone that I should have said, and now I am to write, not one of them will come into my head. Sure as I live it is not settled yet! Good God! the fears and surprises, the crosses and disorders of that day,§ 'twas confused enough to be a dream, and I am apt to think sometimes it was no more. But no, I saw you; when I shall

* For the sake of peace and quiet.   † Deceiving.

‡ This certainly refers to Ireland. Later in this letter Dorothy refers again to a journey Temple was contemplating. He had probably told her during his visit to Chicksands of his intention of going to see his father in Ireland. Dorothy knows how important it is for both of them that Temple's father should be willing to help them.

§ January 13th, when Henry Osborne had returned home to find Temple and Dorothy together. This letter was obviously written in two parts, Dorothy having received a letter from Temple before she had finished hers.

do it again, God only knows! Can there be a more romance story than ours would make if the conclusion should prove happy? Ah! I dare not hope it; something that I cannot describe draws a cloud over all the light my fancy discovers sometimes, and leaves me so in the dark with all my fears about me that I tremble to think on't. But no more of this sad talk.

Who was that Mr. Dr. told you I should marry? I cannot imagine for my life; tell me, or I shall think you made it to excuse yourself. Did not you say once you knew where good French tweezers were to be had? Pray send me a pair; they shall cut no love. Before you go I must have a ring* from you, too, a plain gold one; if I ever marry it shall be my wedding ring; or when I die I'll give it you again. What a dismal story this is you sent me; but who could expect better from a love begun upon such grounds? I cannot pity neither of them, they were both so guilty. Yes, they are the more to be pitied for that.

Here is a note comes to me just now, will you do this service for a fair lady that is my friend;† have not I taught her well, she writes better than her mistress? How merry and pleased she is with her marrying because there is a plentiful fortune; otherwise she would not value the man at all. This is the world; would you and I were out on't: for, sure, we were not made to live in it. Do you remember Herm and the little house there?‡ Shall we go thither? that's next to being out of the world. There we might live like Baucis and Philemon, grow old together in our little cottage, and for our charity to some ship-wrecked strangers obtain the blessing of dying both at the same time. How idly I talk; 'tis because the story pleases me—none in Ovid so much. I remember I cried when I read it. Methought they were the perfectest characters of a contented marriage, where piety and love were all their wealth, and in their poverty feasted the gods when rich men shut them out. I am called away—farewell!

Your faithful.

* This would seem to confirm the fact that during Temple's visit to Chicksands they had reached a new understanding.

† Lady Grey de Ruthin, whose engagement is mentioned in Letter 44. They addressed each other as 'wife' and 'mistress'.

‡ Dorothy and Temple must have seen Herm in 1648 on their way to St Malo, the journey during which they fell in love.

Letter 55

Part of this letter is missing. Dorothy tells Temple about her new admirer, James Beverley, and Lady Grey de Ruthin's account of him. She tells Temple that he must leave for Ireland as soon as possible.

[SATURDAY JANUARY THE 21ST, 1654]

[She did not tell me anything] of what she saw till he was gone, but then I had it in full measure.* 'Tis pity I cannot show you what his wit could do upon so ill a subject, but my Lady Ruthin keeps them to abuse me withal, and has put a tune to them that I may hear them all manner of ways; and yet I do protest I remember nothing more of them than this lame piece:

> *A stately and majestic brow,*
> *Of force to make Protectors bow.*

Indeed, if I have any stately looks I think he has seen them, but yet it seems they could not keep him from playing the fool. My Lady Grey told me that one day talking of me to her (as he would find ways to bring in that discourse by the head and shoulders, whatsoever anybody else could interpose), he said he wondered I did not marry. She (that understood him well enough, but would not seem to do so) said she knew not, unless it were that I liked my present condition so well that I did not care to change it; which she was apt to believe, because to her knowledge I had refused very good fortunes, and named some so far beyond his reach, that she thought she had dashed all his hopes. But he, confident still, said 'twas perhaps that I had no fancy to their persons (as if his own were so taking), that I was to be looked upon as one that had it in my power to please myself, and that perhaps in a person I liked would bate something of fortune. To this my Lady answered again for me, that 'twas not impossible

* 'He' refers almost certainly to James Beverley, a Bedfordshire man who had been at college with Temple. He is mentioned again in Letters 58 and 59.

but I might do so, but in that point she thought me nice and curious* enough. And still to dishearten him the more, she took occasion (upon his naming some gentlemen of the country that had been talked of heretofore as my servants, and are since disposed of) to say (very plainly) that 'twas true they had some of them pretended, but there was an end of my Bedfordshire servants she was sure there were no more that could be admitted into the number. After all this (which would have satisfied an ordinary young man) did I this last Thursday receive a letter from him by Collins, which he sent first to London that it might come from thence to me. I threw it into the fire; and do you but keep my counsel, nobody shall ever know that I had it; and my gentleman shall be kept at such a distance as I hope to hear no more of him. Yet I'll swear of late I have used him so near to rudely that there is little left for me to do. Fye! what a deal of paper I have spent upon this idle fellow; if I had thought his story would have proved so long you should have missed on't, and the loss would not have been great.

I have not thanked you yet for my tweezers and essences; they are both very good. I kept one of the little glasses myself; remember my ring, and in return, if I go to London whilst you are in Ireland, I'll have my picture taken in little and send it you. The sooner you despatch away will be the better, I think, since I have no hopes of seeing you before you go; there lies all your business, your father and fortune must do the rest. I cannot be more yours than I am. You are mistaken if you think I stand in awe of my brother. No, I fear nobody's anger. I am proof against all violence; but when people haunt† me with reasonings and entreaties, when they look sadly‡ and pretend kindness, when they beg upon that score, 'tis a strange pain to me to deny. When he rants and renounces me, I can despise him; but when he asks my pardon, with tears pleads to me the long and constant friendship between us, and calls heaven to witness that nothing upon earth is dear to him in comparison of me, then, I confess, I feel a strange unquietness within me, and I would do anything to avoid his importunity. Nothing is so great a violence to me as that which moves my compassion. I can resist with ease any sort

* Fastidious and exacting.　† Pester.　‡ Look serious, grave.

of people but beggars. If this be a fault in me, 'tis at least a well-natured one; and therefore I hope you will forgive it me, you that can forgive me anything, you say, and be displeased with nothing whilst I love you, may I never be pleased with anything when I do not. Yet I could beat you for writing this last strange letter; was there ever anything said like? If I had not a vanity that the world should admire me, I would not care what they talked of me. In earnest, I believe there is nobody displeased that people speak well of them, and reputation is esteemed by all of much greater value than life itself. Yet let me tell you soberly, that with all my vanity I could be very well contented upon condition nobody should blame me or any action of mine, to quit all my part of the praises and admiration of the world; and if I might be allowed to choose my happiness, part of it should consist in concealment, there should not above two persons in the world know that there was such a one in it as your faithful.

Stay! I have not done yet. Here's another side good, still I find; here, then, I'll tell you that I am not angry for all this. No, I allow it to your ill-humour, and that to the crosses that have been common to us; but now that is cleared up, I shall expect you should say finer things to me. Yet take heed of being like my neighbour's servant,* he is so transported to find no rubs in his way that he knows not whether he stands upon his head or his feet. 'Tis the most troublesome, busy talking little thing that ever was born; his tongue goes like the clack of a mill, but to much less purpose, though if 'twere all oracle, my head would ache to hear that perpetual noise. I admire at her patience and her resolution that can laugh at all his fooleries and love his fortune. You would wonder to see how tired she is with his impertinences,† and yet how pleased she is to think she shall have a great estate with him. But this is the world, and she makes a part of it betimes. Two or three great glistering jewels has bribed her to wink at all his faults, and she hears him as unmoved and unconcerned as if another were to marry him.

What think you, have I not done fair for once, would you wish a longer letter? See how kind I grow at parting; who would not

* Mr Yelverton, the man Lady Grey was going to marry.
† Foolishness.

go into Ireland to have such another? In earnest now, go as soon
as you can, 'twill be the better, I think, who am—Your faithful
friend.

Letter 56

*Temple has taken up one of the themes of the last letter: caring for the
opinion of others. She tells him more about James Beverley, whom Temple
has referred to as a whelp. She sends him a pattern for the ring he is to have
made for her.*

[SATURDAY JANUARY THE 28TH, 1654]

Who would be kind to one that reproaches one so cruelly? Do
you think, in earnest, I could be satisfied the world should think
me a dissembler, full of avarice or ambition? No, you are mistaken; but I'll tell you what I could suffer, that they should say
I married where I had no inclination, because my friends thought
it fit, rather than that I had run wilfully to my own ruin in
pursuit of a fond passion of my own. To marry for love were no
reproachful thing if we did not see that of ten thousand couples
that do it, hardly one can be brought for an example that it may
be done and not repented afterwards. Is there anything thought
so indiscreet, or that makes one more contemptible? 'Tis true
that I do firmly believe we should be, as you say, *tousjours les
mesmes;* but if (as you confess) 'tis that which hardly happens once
in two ages, we are not to expect the world should discern we
were not like the rest. I'll tell you stories another time, you
return them so handsomely upon me. Well, the next servant I
tell you of shall not be called a whelp, if 'twere not to give you a
stick to beat myself with. I would confess that I looked upon the
impudence of this fellow as a punishment upon me for my over
care in avoiding the talk of the world; yet the case is very different, and no woman shall ever be blamed that an inconsiderable
person pretends to her when she gives no allowance* to it, whereas none shall 'scape that owns a passion, though in return of a

* Approval, encouragement.

153

person's much above her. The little tailor that loved Queen Elizabeth was suffered to talk on't and none of her Council thought it necessary to stop his mouth; but the Queen of Sweden's kind letter to the King of Scots* was intercepted by her own ambassador, because he thought it was not for his mistress's honour (at least that was his pretended reason), and thought justifiable enough. But to come to my Beagle again.† I have heard no more of him, though I have seen him since; we met at Wrest again. I do not doubt but I shall be better able to resist his importunity than his tutor was; but what do you think it is that gives him his encouragement? He was told that I had thoughts of marrying a gentleman that had not above two hundred pound a year, only out of a liking to his person. And upon that score his vanity allows him to think he may pretend as far as another. Thus you see 'tis not altogether without reason that I apprehend the noise of the world, since 'tis so much to my disadvantage.

Is it in earnest that you say your being there keeps me from the town? If so, 'tis very unkind. No, if I had gone, it had been to have waited on my neighbour, who has now altered her resolution and goes not herself. I have no business there, and am so little taken with the place that I could sit here seven year without so much as thinking once of going to it. 'Tis not likely, as you say, that you should much persuade your father to what you do not desire he should do; but it is hard if all the testimonies of my kindness are not enough to satisfy without my publishing to the world that I can forget my friends and all my interest to follow my passion; though, perhaps, it will admit of a good sense, 'tis that which nobody but you or I will give it, and we that are concerned in't can only say 'twas an act of great kindness and something romance,‡ but must confess it had nothing of prudence, discretion, nor sober counsel in't. 'Tis not that I expect, by

* Queen Christina, who had succeeded her father in 1632. The future Charles II had been crowned at Scone in January 1651, and was frequently referred to in this way. He had made an offer of marriage to Queen Christina.

† James Beverley, see Letter 55.

‡ Somewhat romantic.

all your father's offers, to bring my friends to approve it. I don't deceive myself thus far, but I would not give them occasion to say that I hid myself from them in the doing it; nor of making my action appear more indiscreet than it is. It will concern me that all the world should know what fortune you have, and upon what terms I marry you, that both may not be made to appear ten times worse than they are. 'Tis the general custom of all people to make those that are rich to have more mines of gold than are in the Indias, and such as have small fortunes to be beggars. If an action take a little in the world, it shall be magnified and brought into comparison with what the heroes or senators of Rome performed; but, on the contrary, if it be once condemned, nothing can be found ill enough to compare it with; and people are in pain till they find out some extravagant expression to represent the folly on't. Only there is this difference, that as all are more forcibly inclined to ill than good, they are much apter to exceed in detraction than in praises. Have I not reason then to desire this from you; and may not my friendship have deserved it? I know not; 'tis as you think; but if I be denied it, you will teach me to consider myself. 'Tis well the side ended here. If I had not had occasion to stop there, I might have gone too far, and showed that I have more passions than one. Yet 'tis fit you should know all my faults, lest you should repent your bargain when 'twill not be in your power to release yourself; besides, I may own my ill-humour to you that cause it; 'tis the discontents my crosses in this business have given me makes me thus peevish. Though I say it myself, before I knew you I was thought as well an humoured young person as most in England; nothing displeased, nothing troubled me. When I came out of France,* nobody knew me again. I was so altered, from a cheerful humour that was always alike, never over merry but always pleased, I was grown heavy and sullen, froward and discomposed; and that country which usually gives people a jolliness and gaiety that is natural to the climate, had wrought in me so contrary effects that I was as new a thing to them as my clothes. If you find all this to be sad truth hereafter, remember that I gave you fair warning.

* Probably refers to her return with her father from France in 1649.

Here is a ring: it must not be at all wider than this, which is rather too big for me than otherwise; but that is a good fault, and counted lucky by superstitious people. I am not so, though: 'tis indifferent to me whether there be any word in't or not; only 'tis as well without, and will make my wearing it the less observed. You must give Nan leave to cut off a lock of your hair for me, too. Oh, my heart! what a sigh was there! I will not tell you how many this journey causes; nor the fears and apprehensions I have for you. No, I long to be rid on you—am afraid you will not go soon enough: do not you believe this? No, my dearest, I know you do not, what'er you say, you cannot doubt but I am

Yours.

Letter 57

Dorothy defends herself for wanting the good opinion of the world. She writes at length on one of her favourite themes: marrying for love and not money. She tells Temple of another argument with her brother. She would like their engagement to remain as secret as possible, and she fears that some of their relations may already have heard of it. She discourses on death, and the general desire not to leave this life.

[SATURDAY FEBRUARY THE 4TH, 1654]

SIR, 'Tis well you have given over your reproaches; I can allow you to tell me of my faults kindly and like a friend. Possibly it is a weakness in me to aim at the world's esteem, as if I could not be happy without it; but there are certain things that custom has made almost of absolute necessity, and reputation I take to be one of those. If one could be invisible I should choose that; but since all people are seen and known, and shall be talked of in spite of their teeth,* who is it that does not desire, at least, that nothing of ill may be said of them, whether justly or otherwise? I never knew any so satisfied with their own innocence as to be content the world should think them guilty. Some out of pride have seemed to contemn ill reports when they have found they

* In spite of all they can do to stop it.

156

could not avoid them, but none out of strength of reason, though many have pretended to it. No, not my Lady Newcastle with all her philosophy, therefore you must not expect it from me. I shall never be ashamed to own that I have a particular value for you above any other, but 'tis not the greatest merit of person will excuse a want of fortune; in some degree I think it will, at least with the most rational part of the world, and, as far as that will reach, I desire it should. I would not have the world believe I married out of interest and to please my friends; I had much rather they should know I chose the person, and took his fortune, because 'twas necessary, and that I prefer a competency with one I esteem infinitely before a vast estate in other hands. 'Tis much easier, sure, to get a good fortune than a good husband; but whosoever marries without any consideration of fortune shall never be allowed to do it out of so reasonable an apprehension,* the whole world (without any reserve) shall pronounce they did it merely to satisfy their giddy humour.

Besides, though you imagine 'twere a great argument of my kindness to consider nothing but you, in earnest I believe 'twould be an injury to you. I do not see that it puts any value upon men when women marry them for love (as they term it); 'tis not their merit, but our folly that is always presumed to cause it; and would it be any advantage to you to have your wife thought an indiscreet person? All this I can say to you; but when my brother disputes it with me I have other arguments for him, and I drove him up so close t'other night that for want of a better gap to get out at he was fain to say that he feared as much your having a fortune as your having none, for he saw you held my Lord Lisle's principles. That religion or honour were things you did not con- sider at all, and that he was confident you would take any engagement, serve in any employment, or do anything to advance yourself. I had no patience for this. To say you were a beggar, your father not worth £4000 in the whole world, was nothing in comparison of having no religion nor no honour. I forgot all my disguise, and we talked ourselves weary; he renounced me again, and I defied him, but both in as civil language as it would permit, and parted in great anger with the usual ceremony of a leg and a

* Shall never be thought to have done it on any such reasonable ground.

courtesy, that you would have died with laughing to have seen us.

The next day I, not being at dinner, saw him not till night; then he came into my chamber, where I supped but he did not. Afterwards Mr. Gibson and he and I talked of indifferent things till all but we two went to bed. Then he sat half-an-hour and said not one word, nor I to him. At last, in a pitiful tone, 'Sister,' says he, 'I have heard you say that when anything troubles you, of all things you apprehend going to bed, because there it increases upon you, and you lie at the mercy of all your sad thoughts, which the silence and darkness of the night adds a horror to; I am at that pass now. I vow to God I would not endure another night like the last to gain a crown.' I, who resolved to take no notice what ailed him, said 'twas a knowledge I had raised from my spleen only, and so fell into a discourse of melancholy and the causes, and from that (I know not how) into religion; and we talked so long of it, and so devoutly, that it laid all our anger. We grew to a calm and peace with all the world. Two hermits conversing in a cell they equally inhabit, never expressed more humble, charitable kindness, one towards another, than we. He asked my pardon and I his, and he has promised me never to speak of it to me whilst he lives, but leave the event to God Almighty; and till he sees it done,* he will be always the same to me that he is; then he shall leave me, he says, not out of want of kindness to me, but because he cannot see the ruin of a person that he loves so passionately, and in whose happiness he had laid up all his. These are the terms we are at, and I am confident he will keep his word with me, so that you have no reason to fear him in any respect; for though he should break his promise, he should never make me break mine. No, let me assure you this rival, nor any other, shall ever alter me, therefore spare your jealousy, or turn it all into kindness.

I will write every week, and no miss of letters shall give us any doubts of one another. Time nor accidents shall not prevail upon our hearts, and, if God Almighty please to bless us, we will meet the same we are, or happier. I will do all you bid me. I will pray, and wish, and hope, but you must do so too, then, and be

* Until he sees that we are married.

so careful of yourself that I may have nothing to reproach you with when you come back.

That vile wench* lets you see all my scribbles, I believe; how do you know I took care your hair should not be spoiled? 'Tis more than ere you did, I think, you are so negligent on't, and keep it so ill, 'tis pity you should have it. May you have better luck in the cutting it than I had with mine. I cut it two or three years agone, and it never grew since. Look to it; if I keep the lock you give me better than you do all the rest, I shall not spare you; expect to be soundly chidden. What do you mean to do with all my letters? Leave them behind you? If you do, it must be in safe hands, some of them concern you, and me, and other people besides us very much, and they will almost load a horse to carry.

Does not my cousins at Moor Park mistrust us a little? I have a great belief they do. I'm sure Robin Cheke told my brother of it since I was last in town. Of all things, I admire my cousin Molle has not got it by the end, he that frequents that family so much, and is at this instant at Kimbolton. If he has, and conceals it, he is very discreet; I could never discern by anything that he knew it. I shall endeavour to accustom myself to the noise on't, and make it as easy to me as I can, though I had much rather it were not talked of till there were an absolute necessity of discovering it, and you can oblige me in nothing more than in concealing it. I take it very kindly that you promise to use all your interest in your father to persuade him to endeavour our happiness, and he appears so confident of his power that it gives me great hopes.

Dear! shall we ever be so happy, think you? Ah! I dare not hope it. Yet 'tis not want of love gives me these fears. No, in earnest, I think (nay, I am sure) I love you more than ever, and 'tis that only gives me these despairing thoughts; when I consider how small a proportion of happiness is allowed in this world, and how great mine would be in a person for whom I have a passionate kindness, and who has the same for me. As it is infinitely above what I can deserve, and more than God Almighty usually allots to the best people, I can find nothing in reason but seems to be against me; and, methinks, 'tis as vain in me to

* Nan.

159

expect it as 'twould be to hope I might be a queen (if that were really as desirable a thing as 'tis thought to be); and it is just it should be so.

We complain of this world, and the variety of crosses and afflictions it abounds in, and yet for all this who is weary on't (more than in discourse), who thinks with pleasure of leaving it, or preparing for the next? We see old folks, that have outlived all the comforts of life, desire to continue it, and nothing can wean us from the folly of preferring a mortal being, subject to great infirmity and unavoidable decays, before an immortal one, and all the glories that are promised with it. Is this not very like preaching? Well, 'tis too good for you; you shall have no more on't. I am afraid you are not mortified enough for such discourses to work upon (though I am not of my brother's opinion, neither, that you have no religion in you). In earnest, I never took anything he ever said half so ill, as nothing, sure, is so great an injury. It must suppose one to be a devil in human shape. Oh, me! now I am speaking of religion, let me ask you is not his name Bagshawe that you say rails on love and women? Because I heard one t'other day speaking of him, and commending his wit, but withal, said he was a perfect atheist. If so, I can allow him to hate us, and love, which, sure, has something of divine in it, since God requires it of us. I am coming into my preaching vein again. What think you, were it not a good way of preferment as the times are? If you advise me to it I'll venture. The woman at Somerset House was cried up mightily. Think on't.

Dear, I am yours.

Letter 58

Dorothy comments on the morals of young people in London now that there is no Court to set them an example. She talks about her latest reading, and tells Temple about a further visit she has received from James Beverley. Temple's father has apparently misunderstood Dorothy's recent attempt to break off their engagement. She praises the lock of Temple's hair she has received.

SIR, The lady was in the right. You are a very pretty gentleman and a modest; were there ever such stories as these you tell? The best on't is, I believe none of them, unless it be that of my Lady Newport, which I must confess is so like her that if it be not true 'twas at least excellently fancied. But my Lord Rich is not caught, though he was near it. My Lady Devonshire, whose daughter his first wife was, has engaged my Lord Warwick to put a stop to the business. Otherwise, I think his present want of fortune, and the little sense of honour he has, might have been prevailed on to marry her.

'Tis strange to see the folly that possesses the young people of this age, and the liberties they take to themselves. I have the charity to believe they appear very much worse than they are, and that the want of a Court to govern themselves by is in great part the cause of their ruin; though that was no perfect school of virtue, yet Vice there wore her mask, and appeared so unlike herself that she gave no scandal. Such as were really as discreet as they seemed to be gave good example, and the eminency of their condition made others strive to imitate them, or at least they durst not own a contrary course. All who had good principles and inclinations were encouraged in them, and such as had neither were forced to put on a handsome disguise that they might not be out of countenance at themselves. 'Tis certain (what you say) that where divine or human laws are not positive we may be our own judges; nobody can hinder us, nor is it in itself to be blamed. But, sure, it is not safe to take all the liberty that is allowed us—there are not many that are sober enough to be trusted with the government of themselves; and because others judge us with more severity than our indulgence to ourselves will permit, it must necessarily follow that 'tis safer being ruled by their opinion than by our own. I am disputing again, though you told me my fault so plainly.

I'll give it over, and tell you that *Parthenissa** is now my company. My brother sent it down, and I have almost read it. 'Tis handsome language; you would know it to be writ by a

---

* A new romance by Lord Broghill. See Letter 40.

person of good quality though you were not told it; but, in the whole, I am not very much taken with it. All the stories have too near a resemblance with those of other romances, there is nothing of new or *surprenant** in them; the ladies are all so kind they make no sport, and I meet only with one that took me by doing a handsome thing of the kind. She was in a besieged town, and persuaded all those of her sex to go out with her to the enemy (which were a barbarous people) and die by their swords, that the provision of the town might last the longer for such as were able to do service in defending it. But how angry was I to see him spoil this again by bringing out a letter this woman left behind her for the governor of the town, where she discovers† a passion for him, and makes *that* the reason why she did it. I confess I have no patience for our *faiseurs de Romance* when they make women court. It will never enter into my head that 'tis possible any woman can love where she is not first loved, and much less that if they should do that, they could have the face to own it. Methinks he that writes *L'illustre Bassa* says well in his epistle that we are not to imagine his hero to be less taking than those of other romances because the ladies do not fall in love with him whether he will or not. 'Twould be an injury to the ladies to suppose they could do so, and a greater to his hero's civility if he should put him upon being cruel to them, since he was to love but one. Another fault I find, too, in the style—'tis affected. *Ambitioned* is a great word with him, and *ignore*; *my concern*, or of *great concern*, is, it seems, properer than *concernment*: and though he makes his people say fine handsome things to one another, yet they are not easy and *naïve* like the French, and there is a little harshness in most of the discourses that one would take to be the fault of a translator rather than of an author. But perhaps I like it the worse for having a piece of *Cyrus* by me that I am hugely pleased with, and that I would fain have you read: I'll send it you. At least read one story that I'll mark you down, if you have time for no more. I am glad you stay to wait on your sister.‡ I would

* Surprising.
† Reveals.
‡ Temple had delayed his departure for Ireland at his father's request, in order to be able to accompany his sister Martha.

162

have my gallant civil to all, much more when it is so due, and kindness too.

I have the cabinet, and 'tis in earnest a pretty one; though you will not own it for a present. I'll keep it as one, and 'tis like to be yours no more but as 'tis mine. I'll warrant you would ne'er have thought of making me a present of charcoal as my servant James* would have done, to warm my heart I think he meant it. But the truth is, I had been inquiring for some (as 'tis a commodity scarce enough in this country), and he hearing of it, told the bailiff he would give him some if 'twere for me. But this is not all. I cannot forbear telling you the other day he made me a visit, and I, to prevent his making discourses to me, made Mrs. Goldsmith and Jane sit by all the while. But he came better provided than I could have imagined. He brought a letter with him, and gave it me as one that he had met with directed to me, he thought it came out of Northamptonshire. I was upon my guard, and suspecting all he said, examined him so strictly where he had it before I would open it, that he was hugely confounded, and I confirmed that 'twas his. I laid it by and wished then they would have left us, that I might have taken notice on't to him. But I had forbid it them so strictly before, that they offered not to stir† farther than to look out at window, as not thinking there was any necessity of giving us their eyes as well as their ears; but he that saw himself discovered took that time to confess to me (in a whispering voice that I could hardly hear myself) that the letter (as my Lord Broghill says) was of *great concern* to him, and begged I would read it, and give him my answer. I took it up presently,‡ as if I had meant it, but threw it, sealed as it was, into the fire, and told him (as softly as he had spoke to me) I thought that the quickest and best way of answering it. He sat awhile in great disorder, without speaking a word, and so rose and took his leave. Now what think you, shall I ever hear of him more?

You do not thank me for using your rival so scurvily nor are not jealous of him, though your father thinks my intentions were not handsome towards you, which methinks is another argument that one is not to be one's own judge; for I am very confident

---

* James Beverley. See Letter 55.   † They made no movement.
‡ Immediately.

they were, and with his favour shall never believe otherwise. I am sure I have no ends to serve of my own in what I did—it could be no advantage to me that had firmly resolved never to marry; but I thought it might be an injury to you to keep you in expectation of what was never likely to be, as I apprehended. Why do I enter into this wrangling discourse? Let your father think me what he pleases, if he ever comes to know me, the rest of my actions shall justify me in this; if he does not, I'll begin to practise upon him* (what you have so often preached to me) to neglect the report of the world, and satisfy myself in my own innocency.

'Twill be pleasinger to you, I am sure, to tell you how fond I am of your lock. Well, in earnest now, and setting aside all compliment, I never saw finer hair, nor of a better colour; but cut no more on't, I would not have it spoiled for the world. If you love me, be careful on't. I am combing, and curling, and kissing this lock all day, and dreaming on't all night. The ring, too, is very well, only a little of the biggest. Send me a tortoise-shell one to keep it on, that is a little less than that I sent for a pattern. I would not have the rule absolutely true without exception that hard hairs are ill natured, for then I should be so. But I can allow that all soft hairs are good, and so are you, or I am deceived as much as you are if you think I do not love you enough. Tell me, my dearest, am I? You will not be if you think I am

Yours.

Letter 59

Dorothy quotes Jeremy Taylor as supporting her belief that it is advisable to resign oneself to the will of another. She looks forward to his journey to Ireland as possibly the last of their separations, and hopes for a good outcome of Temple's attempts to enlist his father's support for their cause.

[SUNDAY FEBRUARY THE 19TH, 1654]

They say you gave order for this vast paper; how do you think

* To put into practice in his case.

I should ever fill it, or with what? I am not always in the humour to wrangle and dispute. For example now, I had rather agree to what you say, than tell you that Dr. Taylor (whose devote you must know I am) says there is a great advantage to be gained in resigning up one's will to the command of another, because the same action which in itself is wholly indifferent, if done upon our own choice, becomes an act of duty and religion if done in obedience to the command of any person whom nature, the laws, or ourselves have given a power over us; so that though in an action already done we can only be our own judges, because we only know with what intentions it was done, yet in any we intend, 'tis safest, sure, to take the advice of another. Let me practise this towards you as well as preach it to you, and I'll lay a wager you will approve on't. But I am chiefly of your opinion that contentment (which the Spanish proverb says is the best paint) gives the lustre to all one's enjoyment, puts a beauty upon things which without it would have none, increases it extremely where 'tis already in some degree, and without it, all that we call happiness besides loses its property. What is contentment, must be left to every particular person to judge for themselves, since they only know what is so to them which differs in all according to their several humours. Only you and I agree 'tis to be found by us in a true friend, a moderate fortune, and a retired life; the last I thank God I have in perfection. My cell is almost finished,* and when you come back you'll find me in it, and bring me both the rest I hope.

I find it much easier to talk of your coming back than you going. You shall never persuade me I send you this journey. No, pray let it be your father's commands, or a necessity your fortune puts upon you. 'Twas unkindly said to tell me I banish you; your heart never told it you, I dare swear; nor mine ne'er thought it. No, my dear, this is, I hope, our last misfortune, let's bear it nobly. Nothing shows we deserve a punishment so much as our murmuring at it; and the way to lessen those we feel, and to 'scape those we fear, is to suffer patiently what is imposed, making a virtue of necessity. 'Tis not that I have less kindness or

* In Letter 57, Dorothy compared her brother and herself to two hermits living together in a cell.

more courage than you, but that mistrusting myself more (as I have more reason) I have armed myself all that is possible against this occasion. I have thought that there is not much difference between your being at Dublin or at London, as our affairs stand. You can write and hear from the first, and I should not see you sooner if you continued still at the last.

Besides, I hope this journey will be of advantage to us; when your father pressed your coming over, he told you you needed not doubt either his power or his will. Have I done anything since that deserves he should alter his intentions towards us? Or has any accident lessened his power? If neither, we may hope to be happy, and the sooner for this journey. I dare not send my boy to meet you at Brickhill nor any other of the servants, they are all too talkative. But I can get Mr. Gibson, if you will, to bring you a letter. 'Tis a civil, well-natured man as can be, of excellent principles and an exact* honesty. I durst make him my confessor, though he is not obliged by his orders to conceal anything that is told him. But you must tell me then which Brickhill 'tis you stop at, Little or Great; they are neither of them far from us. If you stay there you'll write back by him, will you not, a long letter? I shall need it; besides that you owe it me for the last's being so short. Would you saw what letters my brother writes me; you are not half so kind. Well, he is always in the extremes; since our last quarrel he has courted me more than ever he did in his life, and made me more presents, which, considering his humour, is as great a testimony of his kindness as 'twas of Mr. Smith's to my Lady Sunderland when he presented Mrs. Camilla.† He sent me one this week which, in earnest, is as pretty a thing as I have seen, a China trunk, and the finest of the kind that e'er I saw. By the way (this puts me in mind on't), have you read the story of China written by a Portuguese, Fernando Mendez Pinto, I think his name is? If you have not, take it with you, 'tis as diverting a book of the kind as ever I read, and is as handsomely written. You must allow him the privilege of a traveller, and he does not abuse it. His lies are as pleasant harm-

* Perfect.
  † A difficult reference to trace, but it might possibly refer to a present of a mare.

less ones as lies can be, and in no great number considering the scope he has for them. There is one in Dublin now, that ne'er saw much farther, has told me twice as many (I dare swear) of Ireland. If I should ever live to see that country and her in it I should make excellent sport with them. 'Tis a sister of my Lady Grey's, her name is Pooley; her husband lives there too, but I am afraid in no very good condition. They were but poor, and she lived here with her sister when I knew her; 'tis not half a year since she went, I think. If you hear of her, send me word how she makes a shift there.

And hark you, can you tell whether the gentleman that lost a crystal box the 15th of February in St. James' Park or Old Spring Garden* has found it again or not, I have a strange curiosity to know? Tell me, and I'll tell you something that you don't know, which is, that I am your Valentine and you are mine. I did not think of drawing any, but Mrs. Goldsmith and Jane would need make me write some for them and myself; so I writ down our three names, and for men, Mr. Fish,† James B., and you. I cut them all equal and made them up myself before they saw them, and because I would owe it wholly to my good fortune, if I were pleased, I made both them choose first that had never seen what was in them, and they left me you. Then I made them choose again for theirs, and my name was left. You cannot imagine how I was delighted with this little accident, but by taking notice that I cannot forbear telling you it. I was not half so pleased with my encounter next morning. I was up early, but with no design of getting another Valentine, and going out to walk in my night-clothes and night-gown, I met Mr. Fish going a hunting, I think he was; but he stayed to tell me I was his Valentine; and I should not have been rid on him quickly, if he had not thought himself a little too *negligée;* his hair was not powdered, and his clothes were but ordinary; to say truth, he looked then me-thought like other mortal people. Yet he was as handsome as your Valentine. I'll swear you wanted one when you took her, and had very ill fortune that nobody met you before her. Oh, if

* On the edge of the present St James's Park, and belonging to the palace of Whitehall.
† See Letter 26.

167

I had not terrified my little gentleman when he brought me his own letter, how sure I had had him for my Valentine!

On my conscience, I shall follow your counsel if ere he comes again, but I am persuaded he will not. I writ my brother that story for want of something else, and he says I did very well, there was no other way to be rid on him; he makes a remark upon't that I can be severe enough when I please, and wishes I would practise it somewhere else as well as there. Can you tell where that is? I never understand anybody that does not speak plain English, and he never uses that to me of late, but tells me the finest stories (I may apply them how I please) of people that have married where they thought there was great kindness, and how miserably they have found themselves deceived; how despisable they have made themselves by it, and how sadly they have repented it. He reckons more inconveniency than you do that follow good natures, says it makes one credulous, apt to be abused, betrays one to the cunning of people that make advantage on't, and a thousand such things which I hear half asleep and half awake, and take little notice of, unless it be sometimes to say that with all these faults I would not be without it. No, in earnest, nor I could not love any person that I thought had it not to a good degree. 'Twas the first thing I liked in you, and without it I should never have liked anything. I know 'tis counted simple, but I cannot imagine why. 'Tis true some people have it that have not wit, but there are at least as many foolish people that have no good nature, and those are the persons I have ever observed to be fullest of tricks, little ugly plots and designs, unnecessary disguises, and mean cunnings, which are the basest qualities in the world, and makes one the most contemptible, I think; where I once discover them they lose their credit with me for ever. Some will say they are cunning only in their own defence, and that there is no living in this world without it; but I cannot understand how anything more is necessary to one's own safety besides a prudent caution; that I now think is, though I can remember when nobody could have persuaded me that anybody meant ill when it did not appear by their words and actions. I remember my mother (who, if it may be allowed me to say it) was counted as wise a woman as most in England, when she seemed to distrust anybody, and saw I took notice on't, would ask if I did not think her too jealous and a little ill-natured. 'Come, I know you do,' says she, 'if you would confess it, and I cannot blame you. When I was young as you are, I thought my father-in-law (who was a wise man) the most unreasonably suspicious person that ever was, and disliked him for it hugely; but I have lived to see that 'tis almost impossible to think people worse than they are, and so will you.' I did not believe her, and less, that I should have more to say than this paper would hold. It shall never be said I began another at this time of night, though I have spent this idly, that should have told you with a little more circumstance how perfectly

I am yours.

Letter 60

Temple has left for Ireland, and Dorothy says she is sending her letters as usual and presumes arrangements have been made for them to be forwarded to him on the journey. She makes a further reference to one of the causes of their 'quarrel' the previous autumn: the story Temple had heard from a Mr D. She hopes his stay in Ireland will be a short one.

[SATURDAY FEBRUARY THE 25TH, 1654]

You bid me write every week, and I am doing it without considering how it will come to you. Let Nan look to that, with whom, I suppose, you have left the orders of conveyance. I have your last letter; but Jane, to whom you refer me, is not yet come down. On Tuesday I expect her, and if she be not engaged, I shall give her no cause hereafter to believe that she is a burden to me, though I have no employment for her but that of talking to me when I am in the humour of saying nothing. Your dog is come too, and I have received him with all the kindness that is due to anything you send; have defended him from the envy and malice of a troop of greyhounds that used to be in favour with me; and he is so sensible of my care over him, that he is pleased with nobody else, and follows me as if we had been of long acquaintance. 'Tis well you are gone past my recovery. My heart has failed me twenty times since you went, and, had you been within my call, I had brought you back as often, though I know thirty miles' distance and three hundred are the same thing. You will be so kind, I am sure, as to write back by the coach and tell me what the success of your journey so far has been.* After that, I expect no more (unless you stay for a wind) till you arrive at Dublin. I pity your sister in earnest; a sea voyage is welcome to no lady; but you are beaten to it, and 'twill become you, now you are a conductor, to show your valour and keep your company in heart. When do you think of coming back again? I am asking before you are at your journey's end. You will not take it ill that I desire it should be soon. In the meantime, I'll practise all the rules you give me. Who told you I go to bed late? In earnest, they do me wrong: I have been faulty in that point heretofore, I confess, but 'tis a good while since I gave it over with my reading a nights; but in the daytime I cannot live without it, 'tis all my diversion, and infinitely more pleasing to me than any company but yours. And yet I am not given to it in any excess now; I have been very much more. 'Tis Jane, I know, tells all these tales of me. I shall be even with her some time or other, but for the present I long for her with some impatience, that she may tell me all you have told her.

Never trust me if I had not a suspicion from the first that 'twas that ill-looked fellow B—— who made that story Mr. D—— told you.† That which gave me the first inclination to that belief was the circumstance you told me of their seeing me at St. Gregory's. For I remembered to have seen B—— there, and had occasion to look up into the gallery where he sat, to answer a very civil salute given me from thence by Mr. Freeman, and saw B—— in a great whisper with another that sat next him, and pointing to me. If Mr. D—— had not been so nice in discovering his name,‡ you would quickly have been cured of your jealousy. Never believe

* Temple took the coach to Chester; he may have continued to Holyhead, or possibly embarked at Chester for Dublin.
† See Letters 52 and 54.
‡ So scrupulous about revealing his name.

170

I have a servant that I do not tell you of as soon as I know it myself. As, for example now, my brother Peyton has sent to me, for a countryman of his, Sir John Tufton—he married one of my Lady Wotton's daughters and heirs, who is lately dead—and to invite me to think of it. Besides his person and his fortune, without exception, he tells me what an excellent husband he was to this lady that's dead, who was but a crooked, ill-favoured woman, only she brought him £1500 a year. I tell him I believe Sir John Tufton could be content I were so too upon the same terms. But his loving his first wife can be no argument to persuade me; for if he loved her as he ought to do, I cannot hope he should love another so well as I expect anybody should that has me; and if he did not love her, I have less to expect he should me. I do not care for a divided heart; I must have all or none, at least the first place in it. Poor James, I have broke his. He says 'twould pity you to hear what sad complaints he makes; and, but that he has not the heart to hang himself, he could be very well contented to be out of the world.

I have read your wife's letter,* and by it find she has a great deal of wit, though I do not think the manner of her writing very exact; there are many pretty things shuffled together which would do better spoken than in a letter, notwithstanding the received opinion that people ought to write as they speak (which in some sense I think is true). She says, you used to say you loved long letters, which, being spoken without any limitation or qualification, was, in her opinion, a great error, and says she intends your conversion by this long one of hers, and your mortification, too, which is proper this Lent. Asks you if Mrs. Kempston and all her messengers were ever half so troublesome, and whether you do not think it fit to come to composition with her? But yet that you should not think she does this merely to torment you; you are to know that her sister and your cousin Jenny have urged her often to write to you (as not thinking it so

* This is difficult to explain; there is no reference to Temple having enclosed a letter for Dorothy to read, and this may be a playful account of a supposed letter. In Letter 44 Dorothy had said, 'But will not your wife believe . . .', a playful way of referring to someone Temple has been telling her about.

fit for them to do it themselves—one being a widow, and t'other a maid) to reproach your neglect of them. Talks something of the little credit she gives to the report of Mrs. Brookes' and Mrs. Mildmay's reconciliation to their husbands; asks you earnestly whether you were at Mrs. Mildmay's lodging or not, and whether 'tis likely she should ever see the famous beauty you told her of. This is all now; whether any of this be of concernment you can only tell.

That house of your cousin R—— is fatal to physicians. Dr. Smith that took it is dead already; but maybe this was before you went, and so is no news to you. I shall be sending you all I hear; which, though it cannot be much, living as I do, yet it may be more than ventures into Ireland. I would have you diverted, whilst you are there, as much as is possible; but not enough to tempt you to stay one minute longer than your father and your business obliges you. Alas! I have already repented all my share in your journey, and begin to find I am not half so valiant as I sometimes take myself to be. The knowledge that our interests are the same, and that I shall be happy or unfortunate in your person as much or more than in my own, does not give me that confidence you speak of. It rather increases my doubts, and I durst trust your fortune alone, rather than now that mine is joined with it. Yet I will hope yours may be so good as to overcome the ill of mine, and shall endeavour to mend my own all I can by striving to deserve it, maybe, better. My dearest, will you pardon me that I am forced to leave you so soon? The next shall be longer, though I can never be more than I am

Yours.

March was to be an eventful month for Dorothy. Temple was on his way to Ireland, and she was worried for his safety. But Henry Osborne's diary gives us a summary of events:

'March 9th, Thursday. My sister told me she would marry Temple.

'March 11th, being Saturday. My father died just at eleven o'clock of night being within two months 69 years old.

'March 13th. My sister told me she had tied up her hands that she could marry nobody but Temple.'

Letter 61

Dorothy writes of her father's death. She says that her position is now a very difficult one: she has only hostile relations to depend on. She describes her brother's reaction to the news that she is determined to marry Temple, and has committed herself to him. She is unhappy, but there is no danger of her melancholy getting the better of her; she feels strong to face the future.

[MARCH THE 18TH, 1654]*

How true it is that a misfortune never comes single; we live in expectation of some one happiness that we propose to ourselves, an age almost, and perhaps miss it at the last; but sad accidents have wings to overtake us, and come in flocks like ill-boding ravens. You were no sooner gone but (as if that had not been enough) I lost the best father in the world; and though, as to himself, it was an infinite mercy in God Almighty to take him out of a world that can be pleasing to none, and was made more uneasy to him by many infirmities that were upon him, yet to me it is an affliction much greater than people judge it. Besides all that is due to nature and the memory of many (more than ordinary) kindnesses received from him, besides what he was to all that knew him, and what he was to me in particular, I am left by his death in the condition (which of all others) is the most insupportable to my nature, to depend upon kindred that are not friends, and that, though I pay as much as I should do to a stranger,† yet think they do me a courtesy. I expect my eldest brother to-day; if he comes, I shall be able to tell you before I seal up this where you are likely to find me. If he offers me to stay here, this hole will be more agreeable to my humour than any place that is more in the world. I take it kindly that you used arts to conceal our story and satisfy my nice apprehensions, but I'll not impose that constraint upon you any longer, for I find my kind brother publishes it with

---

*This letter, as most that follow are, was dated by Dorothy. It appears as: *March ye 18th* 1653. Dorothy is following the custom of the day, i.e. she considers the New Year to begin on March 25th.

† Dorothy probably paid for her own board and lodging at Chicksands out of her own income.

more earnestness than ever I strove to conceal it; and with more disadvantage than anybody else would. Now he has tried all ways to what he desires, and finds it is vain, he resolves to revenge himself upon me, by representing this action in such colours as will amaze all people that know me, and do not know him enough to discern his malice to me; he is not able to forbear showing it now, when my condition deserves pity from all the world, I think, and that he himself has newly lost a father, as well as I; but takes this time to torment me, which appears (at least to me) so barbarous a cruelty, that though I thank God I have charity enough perfectly to forgive all the injuries he can do me, yet I am afraid I shall never look upon him as a brother more. And now do you judge whether I am not very unhappy, and whether that sadness in my face you used to complain of was not suited to my fortune. You must confess it; and that my kindness for you is beyond example. All these troubles and persecutions that make me weary of the world before my time, cannot lessen the concernment I have for you, and instead of being persuaded, as they would have me, by their malicious stories, methinks I am obliged to love you more in recompense of all the injuries they have done you upon my score. I shall need nothing but my own heart to fortify me in this resolution, and desire nothing in return of it but that your care of yourself may answer that which I shall always have for your interests.

I received your letter of the 10th of this month; and I hope this will find you at your journey's end. In earnest, I have pitied your sister extremely, and can easily apprehend how troublesome this voyage must needs be to her, by knowing what others have been to me; yet, pray assure her I would not scruple at undertaking it myself to gain such an acquaintance, and would go much farther than where (I hope) she now is to serve her. I am afraid she will not think me a fit person to choose for a friend, that cannot agree with my own brother; but I must trust you to tell my story for me, and will hope for a better character from you than he gives me; who, lest I should complain, resolves to prevent* me, and possess† my friends first that he is the injured party. I never magnified my patience to you, but I begin to have

* Forestall.   † Inform.

a good opinion on't since this trial; yet, perhaps, I have no reason, and it may be as well a want of sense in me as of passion; however, you will not be displeased to know that I can endure all that he or anybody else can say, and that setting aside my father's death and your absence, I make nothing an affliction to me, though I am sorry, I confess, to see myself forced to keep such distances with one of his relations, because religion and nature and the custom of the world teaches otherwise. I see I shall not be able to satisfy you in this* how I shall dispose of myself, for my brother is not come; the next will certainly tell you. In the meantime, I expect with great impatience to hear of your safe arrival. 'Twas a disappointment that you missed those fair winds. I pleased myself extremely with a belief that they had made your voyage rather a diversion than a trouble, either to you or your company, but I hope your passage was as happy, if not as sudden† as you expected it; let me hear often from you, and long letters. I do not count this so. Have no apprehensions for me, but all the care of yourself that you please. My melancholy has no danger in't; and I believe the accidents of my life would work more upon any other than they do upon me, whose humour is always more prepared for them than that of gayer persons. I hear nothing that is worth your knowing; when I do, you shall have it. Tell me if there be anything I can do for you, and assure yourself I am perfectly

Yours.

Letter 62

Dorothy has heard from Temple in Dublin. Her engagement to him is now widely known. She is just about to leave for Lady Ruthin's wedding, and tells him about her plans for the coming summer.

[APRIL THE 2ND, 1654]

There was never anybody more surprised than I was with your last. I read it so coldly, and was so troubled to find that you were no forwarder on your journey; but when I came to the last, and saw Dublin at the date, I could scarce believe my eyes. In earnest,

* In this letter.   † Rapid.

it transported me so that I could not forbear expressing my joy in such a manner as had anybody been by to have observed me they would have suspected me no very sober person.

You are safe arrived, you say, and pleased with the place already, only because you meet with a letter of mine there.* In your next I shall expect some other commendations on't, or else I shall hardly make such haste to it as people here believe I will.

All the servants have been to take their leaves on me, and say how sorry they are to hear I am going out of the land; some beggars at the door has made so ill a report of Ireland to them that they pity me extremely, but you are pleased, I hope, to hear I am coming to you; the next fair wind expect me. 'Tis not to be imagined the ridiculous stories they have made, nor how J. B. cries out on me for refusing him and choosing his chamber-fellow†, yet he pities me too, and swears I am condemned to be the miserablest person upon earth. With all his quarrel to me, he does not wish me so ill as to be married to the proudest, imperious, insulting, ill-natured man that ever was; one that before he has had me a week shall use me with contempt, and believe that the favour was of his side. Is not this very comfortable? But, pray, make it no quarrel; I make it none, I can assure you. And though he knew you before I did, I do not think he knows you so well; besides that, his testimony is not of much value.

I am to spend this next week in taking leave of this country, and all the company in't, perhaps never to see it more. From hence I must go into Northamptonshire to see my Lady Ruthin, and so to London, where I shall find my aunt and my brother Peyton, betwixt whom I think to divide this summer.

Nothing has happened since you went worth your knowledge. My Lord Marquis Hertford has lost his eldest son, my Lord Beauchamp, who has left a fine young widow. In earnest, 'tis great pity; at the rate of our young nobility he was an extraordinary person, and remarkable for an excellent husband. My Lord Campden has fought, too, with Mr. Stafford, but there's

* Probably Letter 60, which may have arrived in Dublin before Temple and his sister.

† James Beverley, see Letter 55. He and Temple had been at Emmanuel, Cambridge, together.

176

no harm done. You may discern the haste I'm in by my writing. There will come a time for long letters again, but there will never come any wherein I shall not be

Yours.

FOR MR. WILLIAM TEMPLE,
AT SIR JOHN TEMPLE'S HOUSE
IN DAMASK STREET,
DUBLIN.

Letter 63

[FROM WILLIAM TEMPLE]

There are clearly several letters missing from this time; it is unlikely that six weeks would have passed without some communication between them. This incomplete letter is the only one from Temple to Dorothy during the years before their marriage that has survived. His impatience at being separated from her is evident, as is the sympathy for the lovers felt by Sir John Temple.

[*May* 18*th*, 1654]

This is no artificial humility. I am past all that with you. I know well enough that I am as other people are, but at that rate methinks the world goes, I can see nothing in it to put a value upon besides you; and believe me whatever you have brought me to, and how you have done it, I know not—but I was never intended for that fond thing which people term a lover. I am called upon for my letter, but must have leave first to remember you of yours. For God sake write constantly while I am here, or I am undone past all recovery. I have lived upon them ever since I came, but had thrived much better had they been longer. Unless you use to give me better measure, I shall not be in case to undertake a journey into England. The despair I was in upon the not hearing from you last week, and the belief that all my letters were miscarried (by some treachery among my good friends★ who, I am sorry, have the name of yours), made me press my father by all means imaginable to give me leave to go presently† if I had not heard from you

★ Temple fears that Henry Osborne has again intercepted his letters.
† Immediately.

177

this post. But he would never yield to that, because, he said, upon your silence he should suspect all was not likely to be well between us, and then he was sure I should not be in condition to be alone. He remembered too well the letters I writ upon our last unhappy differences,* and would not trust me from him in such another occasion. But, withal, he told me he would never give me occasion of any discontent which he could remedy; that if you desired my coming over, and I could not be content without, he would not hinder me, though he very much desired my company a month or two longer, and that in that time 'twas very likely I might have his.

Well now, in very good earnest, do you think 'tis time for me to come or no? Would you be very glad to see me there, and could you do it in less disorder, and with less surprise, than you did at Chicksands?†

I ask you these questions very seriously; but yet how willingly would I venture all to be with you. I know you love me still; you have promised it me, and that's all the security I can have for all the good I am ever like to have in this world. 'Tis that which makes all things else seem nothing to it, so high it sets me; and so high indeed, that should I ever fall 'twould dash me all to pieces. Me-thinks your very charity should make you love me more now than ever, by seeing me so much more unhappy than I used, by being so much farther from you, for that is all the measure can be taken of my good or ill condition. Justice, I am sure, will oblige you to it, since you have no other means left in the world of rewarding such a passion as mine, which, sure, is of a much richer value than any-thing in the world besides. Should you save my life again, should you make me absolute master of your fortune and your person too, yet if you loved me not, I should accept none of all this in any part payment, but look upon you as one behindhand‡ with me still. 'Tis no vanity this, but a true sense of how pure and how refined a nature my passion is, which none can ever know besides my own heart, unless you find it out by being there.

* The misunderstanding between them during the previous autumn, resolved in January.
† Temple is referring to his visit to Chicksands on January 13th.
‡ In debt to.

How hard 'tis to think of ending when I am writing to you; but it must be so, and I must ever be subject to other people's occasions, and so never, I think, master of my own. This is too true, both in respect of this fellow's post that is bawling at me for my letter, and of my father's delays. They kill me; but patience—would anybody but I be here! Yet you may command me at one minute's warning. Had I not heard from you by this last, in earnest I had resolved to have gone with this,* and given my father the slip for all his caution. He tells me still of a little time; but, alas! who knows not what mischances and how great changes have often happened in a little time?

For God sake let me know of all your motions,† when and where I may hope to see you. Let us but 'scape this cloud, this absence that has overcast all my contentments, and I am confident there's a clear sky attends us. My dearest dear, adieu. I am

Yours.

Pray, where is your lodging? Have a care of all the despatch and security that can be in our intelligence. Remember [me] to my fellow-servant,‡ sure, by the next I shall write some learned epistle to her, I have been so long about it.

Letter 64

Dorothy is now in London; according to her brother's diary she arrived there on April 20th. He was also in town, and evidently there was much discussion about Temple and her feelings for him.

Dorothy has been greatly comforted by Temple's letter from Ireland, and says she is happy that he has forgiven her brother. She mentions a plot against Cromwell.

[MAY THE 25TH, 1654]

This world is composed of nothing but contrarieties and sudden accidents, only the proportions are not at all equal; for to a great measure of trouble it allows so small a quantity of joy, that one may see 'tis merely intended to keep us alive withal. This is a

* This letter.　　† Plans.
‡ Jane Wright, who was with Dorothy in London.

formal preface, and looks as if there were something of very useful to follow; but I would not wish you to expect it. I was only
considering my own ill-humour last night, I had not heard from
you in a week or more, my brother had been with me and we had
talked ourselves both out of breath and patience too, I was not
very well, and rose this morning only because I was weary of
lying in bed. When I had dined I took a coach and went to see
whether there was ever a letter for me, and was this once so
lucky to find one.* I am not partial to myself I know, and am
contented that the pleasure I have received with this, shall serve
to sweeten many sad thoughts that have interposed since your
last, and more that I may reasonably expect before I have another;
and I think that I may (without vanity) say, that nobody is more
sensible of the least good fortune nor murmurs less at any ill than
I do, since I owe it merely to custom and not to any constancy†
in my humour, or something that is better. No, in earnest, anything of good comes to me like the sun to the inhabitants of
Greenland, it raises them to life when they see it, and when they
miss it, it is not strange they expect a night of half a year long.

You cannot imagine how kindly I take it that you forgive my
brother‡, and let me assure you I shall never press you to anything unreasonable. I will not oblige you to court a person that
has injured you. I only beg that whatsoever he does in that kind
may be excused by his relation to me, and that whensoever you
are moved to think he does you wrong, you will at the same time
remember his sister loves you passionately and nobly; that if he
values nothing but fortune, she despises it, and could love you
as much a beggar as she could do a prince; and shall without
question love you eternally, but whether with any satisfaction to
herself is a sad§ doubt. I am not apt to hope, and whether it be
the better or the worse I know not. All sorts of differences are

* Probably the letter from Dublin, part of which has survived and is
included as Letter 63.

† Courage.

‡ In Letter 63 Temple had suggested that Henry Osborne had tried to
intercept his letters, but in the part of the letter that is missing he had
probably expressed some realization that such interference was under-
standable.

§ Grave.

natural to me, and that which (if your kindness would give you leave) you would term a weakness in me is nothing but a reasonable distrust of my own judgment, which makes me desire the approbation of my friends. I never had the confidence in my life to presume anything well done that I had nobody's opinion in but my own; and as you very well observe, there are so many that think themselves wise when nothing equals their folly but their pride, that I dread nothing so much as discovering such a thought in myself because of the consequences of it.

Whensoever you come you need not doubt your welcome, but I can promise you nothing for the manner on't. I am afraid my surprise and disorder will be more than ever. I have good reasons to think so, and none that you can take ill. But I would not have you attempt it till your father is ready for the journey too. No, really he deserves that all your occasions should wait on his; and if you have not much more than an ordinary obedience for him, I shall never believe you have more than an ordinary kindness for me; since (if you will pardon me the comparison) I believe we both merit it from you upon the same score, he as a very indulgent father, and I as a very kind mistress. Don't laugh at me for commending myself, you will never do it for me, and so I am forced to it.

I am still here in town, but had no hand, I can assure you, in the new discovered plot against the Protector.* But my Lord of Dorchester, they say, has, and so might I have had if I were as rich as he, and then you might have been sure on me at the Tower;—now a worse lodging must serve my turn. 'Tis over against Salisbury House where I have the honour of seeing my Lady M. Sandis every day unless some race or other carry her out of town. The last week she went to one as far as Winchester with Col. Paunton (if you know such a one), and there her husband met her, and because he did so (though it were by accident) thought himself obliged to invite her to his house but seven miles off, and very modestly said no more for it, but that he thought it better than an Inn, or at last a crowded one as all in the town were now because of the race. But she was so good a

* A Royalist plot to assassinate Cromwell on his way to Hampton Court. Many arrests were made. See Letter 70.

companion that she would not forsake her company. So he invited them too, but could prevail with neither. Only my Lady grew kind at parting and said, indeed if Tom Paunton and J. Morton and the rest would have gone she could have been contented to have taken his offer. Thus much for the married people, now for those that are towards it.

There is Mr. Stanley and Mrs. Withrington; Sir H. Littleton and Mrs. Philadelphia Carey, who in earnest is a fine woman, such a one as will make an excellent wife; and some say my Lord Rich and my Lady Betty Howard, but others that pretend to know more say his court to her is but to countenance a more serious one to Mrs. Howard, her sister-in-law, he not having courage to pretend so openly (as some do) to another's wife. Oh, but your old acquaintance, poor Mr. Heningham, has no luck! He was so near (as he thought at last) marrying Mrs. Gerard that anybody might have got his whole estate in wagers upon't that would have ventured but a reasonable proportion of their own. And now he looks more like an ass than ever he did. She has cast him off most unhandsomely, that's the truth on't, and would have tied him to such conditions as he might have been her slave with but could never be her husband. Is not this a great deal of news for me that never stir abroad? Nay, I had brought me to-day more than all this: that I am marrying myself! And the pleasantness on't is that it should be to my Lord St. John. Would he look on me, think you, that had pretty Mrs. Frescheville? My comfort is, I have not seen him since he was a widower, and never spoke to him in my life. I found myself so innocent that I never blushed when they told it me. What would I give I could avoid it when people speak of you? In earnest, I do prepare myself all that is possible to hear it spoken of, yet for my life I cannot hear your name without discovering* that I am more than ordinarily concerned in't. A blush is the foolishest thing that can be, and betrays one more than a red nose does a drunkard; and yet I would not so wholly have lost them as some women that I know has, as much injury as they do me.

I can assure you now that I shall be here a fortnight longer (they tell me no lodger, upon pain of his Highness's displeasure,

* Revealing.

182

must remove sooner);* but when I may have his leave I go into Suffolk for a month, and then come hither again to go into Kent, where I intend to bury myself alive again as I did in Bedfordshire, unless you call me out and tell me I may be happy. Alas! how fain I would hope it, but I cannot, and should it ever happen, 'twould be long before I should believe 'twas meant for me in earnest, or that 'twas other than a dream. To say truth, I do not love to think on't, I find so many things to fear and so few to hope.

'Tis better telling you that I will send my letters where you direct, that they shall be as long ones as possibly my time will permit, and when at any time you miss of one, I give you leave to imagine as many kind things as you please, and to believe I mean them all to you.

Farewell.

Letter 65

A letter from Temple has gone astray. Dorothy is very upset to learn of his father's illness.

JUNE THE 6TH, 1654

I see you know how to punish me. In earnest, I was so frighted with your short letter as you cannot imagine, and as much troubled at the cause on't. What is it your father ails, and how long has he been ill? If my prayers are heard, he will not be so long. Why do you say I failed you? Indeed, I did not. Jane is my witness. She carried my letter to the White Hart, by St. James's, and 'twas a very long one too. I carried one thither since, myself, and the woman of the house was so very angry, because I desired her to have a care on't, that I made the coachman drive with all possible speed, lest she should have beaten me. To say truth, I pressed her too much, considering how little the letter deserved it. 'Twas writ in such disorder, the company prating about me,

* As a result of the discovery of the plot against Cromwell a proclamation was issued on May 23rd forbidding all persons temporarily in London to leave the city.

and some of them so bent on doing me little mischiefs, that I knew not what I did, and believe it was the most senseless, disjointed thing that ever was read.

I remember now that I writ Robin Spencer instead of Will. 'Tis he that has married Mrs. Gerard, and I admire their courages. She will have six hundred pounds a year, 'tis true, after her mother; but how they will live till then I cannot imagine. I shall be even with you for your short letter. I'll swear they will not allow me time for anything, and to show how absolutely I am governed I need but tell you that I am every night in the Park and at New Spring Garden,* where, though I come with a mask, I cannot scape being known, nor my conversion being admired. Are not you in some fear what will become on me? These are dangerous courses. I do not find, though, that they have altered me yet. I am much the same person I was, at least in being

Yours.

Letter 66

Dorothy announces her departure from London. She promises to arrange to have a miniature made for Temple.

[TUESDAY] JUNE 13TH [1654]

You have satisfied me very much with this last long letter, and made some amends for the short one I received before. I am convinced, too, happiness is much such a kind of thing as you describe, or rather such a nothing. For there is no one thing can properly be called so, but every one is left to create it to themselves in something which they either have or would have; and so far it's well enough. But I do not like that one's happiness should depend upon a persuasion that this is happiness, because nobody knows how long they shall continue in a belief built upon no grounds, only to bring it to what you say, and to make it absolutely of the same nature with faith. We must conclude that

* Was at Lambeth, and later became known as Vauxhall Gardens; Old Spring Garden was originally on the edge of the present St James's Park.

nobody can either create or continue such a belief in themselves; but where it is there is happiness. And for my part at this present, I verily believe I could find it in the long walk at Dublin.

You say nothing of your father's sickness, therefore I will hope he is well again; for though I have a quarrel to him, it does not extend so far as to wish him ill. But he made no good return for the counsel I gave you, to say that there might come a time when my kindness might fail. Do not believe him, I charge you, unless you doubt yourself that you may give me occasion to change; and when he tells you so again, engage what you please upon't, and put it upon my account. I shall go out of town this week, and so cannot possibly get a picture drawn for you till I come up again, which will be within these six weeks, but not to make any stay at all. I should be glad to find you here then. I would have had one drawn since I came, and consulted my glass every morning when to begin; and to speak freely to you that are my friend, I could never find my face in a condition to admit on't, and when I was not satisfied with it myself, I had no reason to hope that anybody else should. But I am afraid, as you say, that time will not mend it, and therefore you shall have it as it is as soon as Mr. Cooper will vouchsafe to take the pains to draw it for you. I have made him twenty courtesies, and promised him £15 to persuade him.

I am in great trouble to think how I shall write out of Suffolk to you, or receive yours. However, do not fail to write, though they lie awhile. I shall have them at last, and they will not be the less welcome; and, though you should miss of some of mine, let it not trouble you; but if it be my fault, I'll give you leave to demand satisfaction for it when you come. Jane kisses your hands, and says she will be ready in all places to do you service; but I'll prevent her, now you have put me into a jealous humour. I'll keep her in chains before she shall quit scores with me. Do not believe, sir, I beseech you, that the young heirs are for you; content yourself with your old mistress. You are not so handsome as Will Spencer, nor I have not so much courage nor wealth as his mistress, nor she has not so much as her aunt says by all the money. I should not have called her his mistress now they have been married almost this fortnight.

I'll write again before I leave the town, and should have writ more now, but company is come in. Adieu, my dearest.

Letter 67

Dorothy says she does not like the idea of an elaborate wedding. Sir John Temple and Sir Thomas Peyton are to negotiate the marriage treaty, so it is evident that the possibility of Dorothy and William getting married was becoming more and more of a reality.

[THURSDAY JUNE THE 15TH, 1654]

I promised in my last to write again before I went out of town, and now I'll be as good as my word. They are all gone this morning,* and have left me much more at liberty than I have been of late, therefore I believe this will be a long letter; perhaps too long, at least if my letters are as little entertaining as my company is. I was carried yesterday abroad to a dinner† that was designed for mirth, but it seems one ill-humoured person in the company is enough to put all the rest out of tune; for I never saw people perform what they intended worse, and could not forbear telling them so; but to excuse themselves and silence my reproaches, they all agreed to say that I spoiled their jollity by wearing the most unseasonable looks that could be put on for such an occasion. I told them I knew no remedy but leaving me behind next time, and could have told them that my looks were suitable to my fortune, though not to a feast. Fye! I am got into my complaining humour that tires myself as well as everybody else, and which (as you observe) helps not at all. Would it would leave me, and that I could believe I shall not always have occasion for it. But that's in nobody's power, and my Lady Talmash, that

* Henry Osborne's diary fixes the date of this letter; he says that on that day Dorothy moved from Lady Ruthin's in Queen Street to Drury Lane. It was Lady Ruthin's party that left London.

† Henry Osborne writes: 'My aunt Gargrave and my cousin Thorold, my sister and I dined at the Swan in Fish Street, my sister and I had the great falling out and were friends again.' Dorothy's nervous condition was undoubtedly a result of the negotiations about her marriage.

186

says she can do whatsoever she will, cannot believe whatsoever she pleases. 'Tis not unpleasant, methinks, to hear her talk, how at such a time she was sick and the physicians told her she would have the small-pox, and showed her where they were coming out upon her; but she bethought herself that it was not at all convenient for her to have them at that time; some business she had that required her going abroad; and so she resolved she would not be sick, nor was not. Twenty such stories as these she tells; and then falls into discourses of the strength of reason and the power of philosophy, till she confounds herself and all that hear her. You have no such ladies in Ireland?

Oh me, but I heard to-day your cousin Hammond is going thither to be in Ludlow's place.* Is it true? You tell me nothing what is done there, but 'tis no matter. The less one knows of state affairs I find it is the better. My poor Lady Vavasour is carried to the Tower, and her great belly could not excuse her, because she was acquainted that there was a plot against the Protector, and did not discover it. She has told now all that was told her, but vows she will never say from whence she had it: we shall see whether her resolutions are as unalterable as those of my Lady Talmash. I wonder how she behaved herself when she was married. I never saw any one yet that did not look simply and out of countenance, nor ever knew a wedding well designed but one; and that was of two persons who had time enough I confess to contrive it, and nobody to please in't but themselves. He came down into the country where she was upon a visit, and one morning married her. As soon as they came out of the church they took coach and came for the town, dined at an inn by the way, and at night came into lodgings that were provided for them where nobody knew them, and where they passed for married people of seven years' standing.

The truth is I could not endure to be Mrs. Bride in a public wedding, to be made the happiest person on earth. Do not take it ill, for I would endure it if I could, rather than fail; but in earnest I do not think it were possible for me. You cannot apprehend the

* Colonel Robert Hammond was appointed a member of the Irish Council in August. He died early in October. Ludlow had resigned in April 1654.

formalities of a treaty more than I do, nor so much the success on't. Yet in earnest, your father will not find my brother Peyton wanting in civility (though he is not a man of much compliment, unless it be in his letters to me), nor an unreasonable person in anything, so he will allow him out of kindness to his wife to set a higher value upon her sister than she deserves. I know not how he may be prejudiced as to the business, but he is not deaf to reason when 'tis civilly delivered, and is as easily gained with compliance and good usage as anybody I know, but by no other way. When he is roughly dealt with, he is like me, ten times the worse for't.

I make it a case of conscience to discover* my faults to you as fast as I know them, that you may consider what you have to do. My aunt told me no longer agone than yesterday that I was the most wilful woman that ever she knew, and had an obstinacy of spirit nothing could overcome. Take heed! you see I give you fair warning.

I have missed a letter this Monday. What is the reason? By the next, I shall be gone into Kent, and my other journey is laid aside,† which I am not displeased at, because it would have broken our intercourse very much.

Here are some verses of Cowley's.‡ Tell me how you like them. 'Tis only a piece taken out of a new thing of his; the whole is very long, and is a description of, or rather a paraphrase upon, the friendships of David and Jonathan. 'Tis, I think, the best I have seen of his, and I like the subject because 'tis that I would be perfect in

Adieu. Je suis vostre.

Letter 68

Dorothy is about to leave for Kent to stay with her brother-in-law, Sir Thomas Peyton. She has decided to go by water to Gravesend. She mentions

* Reveal.

† The visit she had intended to pay in Suffolk. She is to go to her brother-in-law, Sir Thomas Peyton, in Kent.

‡ Abraham Cowley's *Davideis*. Dorothy had probably read them in manuscript as they were not published until 1656.

a servant she has already recommended to Temple, but the original recom-
mendation must have been in a letter that has been lost.

JUNE THE 26TH [1654]

I told you in my last that my Suffolk journey was laid aside, and
that into Kent hastened. I am beginning it to-day; and have
chosen to go as far as Gravesend by water, though it be very
gloomy weather. If I drown by the way, this will be my last
letter; and, like a will, I bequeath all my kindness to you in it,
with a charge never to bestow it all upon another mistress, lest
my ghost rise again and haunt you. I am in such haste that I
can say little else to you now. When you are come over, we'll
think where to meet, for at this distance I can design nothing;
only I should be as little pleased with the constraint of my
brother's house as you. Pray let me know whether your man
leaves you, and how you stand inclined to him I offer you.
Indeed, I like him extremely, and he is commended to me, by
people that know him very well and are able to judge, for a most
excellent servant, and faithful as possible. I'll keep him unengaged
till I hear from you. Adieu.

My next shall make amends for this short one.

[P.S.]—I received your last of June 22nd since I sealed up my
letter, and I durst not but make an excuse for another short one,
after you have chid me so for those you have received already;
indeed, I could not help it, nor cannot now, but if that will
satisfy I can assure you I shall make a much better wife than I do
a husband,* if I ever am one. *Pardon, mon Cher Cœur, on m'attend.*
Adieu, mon Ame.   Je vous souhait tout ce que vous desiré.

Letter 69

*Dorothy writes from Knowlton in Kent. The house is crowded, and she
has little time for writing letters.*

* Probably used in the sense of 'an economical person'.

Because you find fault with my other letters, this is like to be shorter than they; I did not intend it so though, I can assure you. But last night my brother† told me he did not send his till ten o'clock this morning, and now he calls for mine at seven, before I am up; and I can only be allowed time to tell you that I am in Kent, and in a house so strangely crowded with company, that I am weary as a dog already, though I have been here but three or four days; that all their mirth has not mended my humour, and that I am here the same I was in other places; that I hope, merely because you bid me, and lose that hope as often as I consider anything but yours. Would I were easy of belief! they say one is so to all that one desires. I do not find it, though I am told I was so extremely when I believed you loved me. That I would not find, and you have only power to make me think it. But I am called upon. How fain I would say more; yet 'tis all but the saying with more circumstance that I am

Yours.

FOR YOUR MASTER.

Letter 70

Dorothy is sorry to hear that Temple has already engaged a servant and that her recommendation came too late. She complains of his short letters. She looks forward to his return from Ireland.

JULY THE 10TH [1654]

I am very sorry I spoke too late, for I am confident this was an excellent servant. He was in the same house where I lay, and I had taken a great fancy to him, upon what was told me of him

---

* Although this letter is dated June, it undoubtedly was July; Dorothy probably made the mistake owing to the haste with which she was writing.

† Henry Osborne was at Knowlton from June 27th until July 13th.

and what I saw. The poor fellow, too, was so pleased that I undertook to inquire out a place for him, that, though mine was, as I told him, uncertain, yet upon the bare hopes on't he refused two or three good conditions; but I shall set him now at liberty, and not think at all the worse of him for his good-nature. Sure you go a little too far in your condemnation on't. I know it may be abused, as the best things are most subject to be, but in itself 'tis so absolutely necessary that where it is wanting nothing can recompense the miss on't. The most contemptible person in the world, if he has that, cannot be justly hated, and the most considerable without it cannot deserve to be loved. Would to God I had all that good-nature you complain you have too much of, I could find ways enough to dispose on't amongst myself and my friends; but 'tis well where it is, and I should sooner wish you more on't than less.

I wonder with what confidence you can complain of my short letters that are so guilty yourself in the same kind. I have not seen a letter this month that has been above half a sheet. Never trust me if I write more than you that live in a desolated country where you might finish a romance of ten tomes before anybody interrupted you—I that live in a house the most filled of any since the Ark, and where, I can assure [you], one has hardly time for the most necessary occasions. Well, there was never any one thing so much desired and apprehended at the same time as your return is by me; it will certainly, I think, conclude me a very happy or a most unfortunate person. Sometimes, methinks, I would fain know my doom whatever it be; and at others, I dread it so extremely, that I am confident the five Portugals and the three plotters which were t'other day condemned* by the High Courts of Justice had not half my fears upon them. I leave you to judge the constraint I live in, what alarms my thoughts give me, and yet how unconcerned this company requires I should be; they

* Dom Pantaleon, brother of the Portuguese ambassador, had insisted that he had been insulted by Colonel Gerard, a young Royalist, and had engineered a fight with him. In the course of the scuffle an onlooker had been shot. Pantaleon and his associates were tried and condemned to death. Gerard was beheaded at the Tower with Pantaleon, having been convicted for his part in the plot against the Protector.

will have me act my part in a play, 'The Lost Lady' it is, and I am she. Pray God it be not an ill omen!

I shall lose my eyes and you this letter if I make it longer. Farewell.

I am,
Yours.

Letter 71

Temple has been worried by Letter 68 in which Dorothy said she was leaving for Kent by boat. He has not yet received her letter of July 4th. A lady has urged her never to marry.

[SATURDAY JULY THE 15TH, 1654]

I see you can chide when you please, and with authority; but I deserve it, I confess, and all I can say for myself is, that my fault proceeded from a very good principle in me. I am apt to speak what I think; and to you have so accustomed myself to discover all my heart that I do not believe 'twill ever be in my power to conceal a thought from you. Therefore I am afraid you must resolve to be vexed with all my senseless apprehensions as my brother Peyton is with some of his wife's, who is, though, a very good woman, but the most troublesome one in a coach that ever was. We dare not let our tongues lie more on one side of our mouths than t'other for fear of overturning it. You are satisfied, I hope, ere this that I 'scaped drowning. However, 'tis not amiss that my will is made? You know now how to dispose of all my wealth whensoever I die. But I am troubled much you should make an ill journey to so little purpose; indeed, I writ by the first post after my arrival here, and cannot imagine how you came to miss of my letter. Is your father returned yet, and do you think of coming over immediately? How welcome you will be. But alas! I cannot talk on't at the rate that you do. I am sensible that such an absence is misfortune enough, but I dare not promise myself that it will conclude ours; and 'tis more my belief that you yourself speak it rather to encourage me, and to show your wishes than your hopes.

192

My humour is so ill at present, that I dare say no more lest you should chide again. I find myself fit for nothing but to converse with a lady below, that is fallen out with all the world because her husband and she cannot agree. 'Tis the pleasantest thing that can be to hear us discourse. She takes great pains to dissuade me from ever marrying, and says I am the veriest fool that ever lived if I do not take her counsel. Now we do not absolutely agree in that point, but I promise her never to marry unless I can find such a husband as I describe to her, and she believes is never to be found; so that, upon the matter, we differ very little, and whensoever she is accused of maintaining opinions very destructive of society, and absolutely prejudicial to all the young people of both sexes that live in the house, she calls out me to be her second, and by it has lost me the favour of all our young gallants, who have got a custom of expressing anything that is nowhere but in fiction by the name of 'Mrs. O——'s husband.' For my life I cannot beat into their heads a passion that must be subject to no decay, an even perfect kindness that must last perpetually, without the least intermission. They laugh to hear me say that one unkind word would destroy all the satisfaction of my life, and that I should expect our kindness should increase every day, if it were possible, but never lessen. All this is perfect nonsense in their opinion; but I should not doubt the convincing them if I could hope I should ever be so happy as to be

Yours.

Letter 72

Dorothy describes her life at Knowlton. She tells him of a visit she paid to Lilly the astrologer just before leaving London.

[SATURDAY JULY 22ND, 1654]

How long this letter will be I cannot tell. You shall have all the time that is allowed me, but upon condition that you shall not examine the sense on't too strictly, for you must know I want sleep extremely. The sun was up an hour before I went to bed to-day, and this is not the first time I have done this since I came hither. 'Twill not be for your advantage that I should stay here long; for, in earnest, I shall be good for nothing if I do. We go abroad all day and play all night, and say our prayers when we have time. Well, in sober earnest now, I would not live thus a twelvemonth to gain all that the King★ has lost, unless it were to give it him again. 'Tis a miracle to me how my brother† endures it. 'Tis as contrary to his humour as darkness is to light, and only shows the power he lets his wife have over him. Will you be so good-natured? He has certainly as great a kindness for her as can be, and, to say truth, not without reason; but of all the people that ever I saw, I do not like his carriage towards her. He is perpetually wrangling and finding fault, and to a person that did not know him would appear the worst husband and the most imperious in the world. He is so amongst his children too, though he loves them passionately. He has one son, and 'tis the finest boy that e'er you saw, and has a notable spirit, but yet stands in that awe of his father that one word from him is as much as twenty whippings.

You must give me leave to entertain you thus with discourses of the family, for I can tell you nothing else from hence. Yet, now I remember, I have another story for you. You little think I have been with Lilly; in earnest, I was, the day before I came out of town; and what do you think I went for? Not to know when you would come home, I can assure you, nor for any other occasion of my own; but with a cousin of mine that had long designed to make herself sport with him, and did not miss of her aim. I confess I always thought him an impostor, but I could never have imagined him so simple a one as we found him. In my life I never heard so ridiculous a discourse as he made us, and no old woman that passes for a witch could have been more to seek what to say to reasonable people than he was. He asked us more questions than we did him, and caught at everything we said without discerning that we abused him and said things purposely

★ Dorothy is quite at ease in expressing her Royalist sympathies to Temple by referring to the exiled Charles Stuart as the King. He was already acknowledged as Charles II by Royalists.

† Sir Thomas Peyton, her brother-in-law.

to confound him; which we did so perfectly that we made him contradict himself the strangest that ever you heard. Ever since this adventure, I have had so great a belief in all things of this nature, that I could not forbear laying a peascod with nine peas in't under the door yesterday, and was informed by it that my husband's name should be Thomas. How do you like that? But what Thomas, I cannot imagine, for of all the servants I have got since I came hither I know none of that name.

Here is a new song—I do not send it to you but to your sister; the tune is not worth the sending so far. If she pleases to put any to it, I am sure it will be a better than it has here.

Adieu.

Letter 73

Temple is about to leave Ireland for England. She wishes his journey were over. She tells him more of life at Knowlton, which is not to her liking.

[SATURDAY SEPTEMBER THE 2ND, 1654]

I wonder you did not come before your last letter. 'Twas dated the 24th of August, but I received it not till the 1st of September. Would to God your journey were over! Every little storm of wind frights me so, that I pass here for the greatest coward that ever was born, though, in earnest, I think I am as little so as most women, yet I may be deceived, too, for now I remember me you have often told me I was one, and, sure, you know what kind of heart mine is better than anybody else.

I am glad you are pleased with that description* I made you of my humour, for, though you had disliked it, I am afraid 'tis past my power to help. You need not make excuses neither for yours; no other would please me half so well. That gaiety which you say is only esteemed would be insupportable to me, and I can as little endure a tongue that's always in motion as I could the clack of a mill. Of all the company this place is stored with, there is but two persons whose conversation is at all easy to me;

* Dorothy is referring to a letter which has not survived.

195

one is my eldest niece, who, sure, was sent into the world to show 'tis possible for a woman to be silent; the other is a gentleman whose mistress died just when they should have married; and though 'tis many years since, one may read it in his face still. His humour was very good, I believe, before that accident,* for he will yet say things pleasant enough, but 'tis so seldom that he speaks at all, and when he does 'tis with so sober a look, that one may see he is not moved at all himself when he diverts the company most. You will not be jealous though I say I like him very much. If you were not secure in me, you might be so in him. He would expect his mistress should rise again to reproach his inconstancy if he made court to anything but her memory. Methinks we three (that is, my niece, and he and I) do become this house the worst that can be, unless I should take into the number my brother Peyton himself too; for to say truth his, for another sort of melancholy, is not less than ours. What can you imagine we did this last week, when to our constant company there was added a colonel and his lady, a son of his and two daughters, a maid of honour to the Queen of Bohemia, and another colonel or a major, I know not which, besides all the train they brought with them; the men the greatest drinkers that ever I saw, which did not at all agree with my brother, who would not be drawn to it to save a kingdom if it lay at stake and no other way to redeem it? But, in earnest, there was one more to be pitied besides us, and that was Colonel Thornhill's wife, as pretty a young woman as I have seen. She is Sir John Grenville's sister, and has all his good-nature, with a great deal of beauty and modesty, and wit enough. This innocent creature is sacrificed to the veriest beast that ever was. The first day she came hither he intended, it seems, to have come with her, but by the way called in to see an old acquaintance, and bid her go on, he would overtake her, but did not come till next night after, and then so drunk that he was laid immediately to bed, whither she was to follow him when she had supped. I blest myself at her patience, as you may do that I could find anything to fill up this paper withal.

Adieu.

* Occurrence.

Letter 74

Dorothy is relieved to know that Temple has arrived safely in London. She wonders why he has not yet come down to Knowlton.

[SATURDAY SEPTEMBER THE 9TH, 1654]

I did so promise myself a letter on Friday that I am very angry I had it not, though I know you were not come to town when it should have been writ. But did not you tell me you should not stay a day or two? What is it that has kept you longer? I am pleased, though, to know that you are out of the power of so uncertain things as the winds and the sea, which I never feared for myself, but did extremely apprehend for you. You will find a packet of letters to read, and maybe have met with them already. If you have, you are so tired that 'tis reasonable I should spare you in this. To say truth, I have not time to make this longer; besides that if I had, my pen is so very good that [it] writes an invisible hand, I think; I am sure I cannot read it myself. If your eyes are better, you will find that I intended to assure you

I am yours.

Letter 75

Dorothy insists again that her love for Temple is not dependent on his fortune. She hopes his father will consent to negotiate the marriage treaty with her brother Henry. If anything is to come of their relationship, his father must forget Henry's earlier attitude to him.

[SATURDAY SEPTEMBER THE 16TH, 1654]

I am but newly waked out of an unquiet sleep, and I find it so late that if I write at all it must be now. Some company that was here last night kept us up till three a clock, and then we lay three in a bed, which was all one to me as if we had not gone at all. Since dinner they are all gone, and our company with them part of the way, and with much ado I got to be excused, that I might recover a little sleep, but am so moped yet that, sure, this letter will be nonsense.

I would fain tell you, though, that your father is mistaken, and that you are not, if you believe that I have all the kindness and tenderness for you my heart is capable of. Let me assure you (whate'er your father thinks) that had you £20,000 a year I could love you no more than I do, and should be far from showing it so much lest it should look like a desire of your fortune, which, as to myself, I value as little as anybody breathing. I have not lived thus long in the world, and in this age of changes, but certainly I know what an estate is. I have seen my father's reduced, better than £4000, to not £400 a year, and I thank God I never felt the change in anything that I thought necessary. I never wanted, nor am confident I never shall. But yet, I would not be thought so inconsiderate a person as not [to] remember that it is expected from all people that have sense that they should act with reason, that to all persons some proportion of fortune is necessary, according to their several qualities, and though it is not required that one should tie oneself to just so much, and something is left for one's inclination, and the difference in the persons to make, yet still within such a compass, —and such as lay more upon those considerations than they will bear, shall infallibly be condemned by all sober persons. If any accident out of my power should bring me to necessity though never so great, I should not doubt with God's assistance but to bear it as well as anybody, and I should never be ashamed on't if He pleased to send it me; but if by my own folly I had put it upon myself, the case would be extremely altered. If ever this comes to a treaty, I shall declare that in my own choice I prefer you much before any other person in the world, and all that this inclination in me (in the judgments of any persons of honour and discretion) will bear, I shall desire may be laid upon it to the uttermost of what they can allow. And if your father please to make up the rest, I know nothing that is like to hinder me from being yours. But if your father, out of humour, shall refuse to treat with such friends as I have, let them be what they will, it must end here; for though I was content, for your sake, to lose them, and all the respect they had for me, yet, now I have done that, I'll never let them see that I have so little interest in you and yours as not to prevail that my brother may be admitted to treat for me. Sure, when a thing of course and so much reason as that (unless I did declare to all the world he were my enemy), it must be expected whensoever I dispose of myself he should be made no stranger to it. When that shall be refused me, I may be justly reproached that I deceived myself when I expected to be at all valued in a family that I am a stranger to, or that I should be considered with any respect because I had a kindness for you, that made me not value my own interests.

I doubt much whether all this be sense or not; I find my head so heavy. But that which I would say is, in short, this: if I did say once that my brother should have nothing to do in't, 'twas when his carriage towards me gave me such an occasion as could justify the keeping that distance with him; but now it would look extremely unhandsome in me, and, sure, I hope your father would not require it of me. If he does, I must conclude he has no value for me, and, sure, I never disobliged him to my knowledge, and should, with all the willingness imaginable, serve if it lay in my power.

Good God! what an unhappy person am I. But all the world is so almost. Just now they are telling me of a gentleman near us that is the most wretched creature made (by the loss of a wife that he passionately loved) that can be. If your father would but in some measure satisfy my friends that I might but do it in any justifiable manner, you should dispose me as you pleased, carry me whither you would, all places of the world would be alike to me where you were, and I should not despair of carrying myself so towards him as might deserve a better opinion from him.

I am yours.

Letter 76

Dorothy gives Temple reasons for his father agreeing to her brother Henry joining Sir Thomas Peyton in the marriage-treaty negotiations; Peyton will not act without consulting Henry, in any case. She implies

*that Sir John has already agreed, but has been annoyed by a reference to
an earlier stage in their relationship.*

My doubts and fears were not at all increased by that which
gives you so many, nor did I apprehend* that your father might
not have been prevailed with to have allowed my brother's being
seen in the treaty; for as to the thing itself, whether he appears in't
or not, 'twill be the same. He cannot but conclude my brother
Peyton would not do anything in it without the others' consent.

I do not pretend to any share in your father's kindness, as
having nothing in me to merit it; but as much a stranger as I am
to him, I should have taken it very ill if I had desired it of him,
and he had refused it me. I do not believe my brother has said
anything to his prejudice, unless it were in his persuasions to me,
and there it did not injure him at all. If he takes it ill that my
brother appears so very averse to the match, I may do so too,
that he was the same; and nothing less than my kindness for you
could have made me take so patiently as I did his saying to some
that knew me at York† that he was forced to bring you thither
and afterwards to send you over lest you should have married
me. This was not much to my advantage, nor hardly civil, I
think, to any woman; yet I never so much as took the least
notice on't, nor had not now, but for this occasion; yet, sure, it
concerns me to be at least as nice as he in point of honour. I think
'tis best for me to end here lest my anger should make me lose
that respect I would always have for your father, and 'twere not
amiss, I think, that I diverted it all towards you for being so idle
as to run out of your bed to catch such a cold.

If you come hither you must expect to be chidden so much
that you will wish you had stayed till we came up, when perhaps
I might have almost forgot half my quarrel to you. At this present
I can assure you I am pleased with nobody but your sister, and
her I love extremely, and will call her pretty; say what you will,
I know she must be so, though I never saw more of her than what

* Fear.

† This probably refers to the summer of 1651, when Temple was
ordered to meet his father in York and go from there to the Low Countries.

200

her letters show. She shall have two spots* if she please (for I had just such another given me after you were gone), or anything else that is in the power of

Your.

Letter 77

Dorothy asks Temple to come and see her at Knowlton. She is anxious to hear what action his father is going to take on their behalf.

MONDAY OCTOBER THE 2ND [1654]

After a long debate with myself how to satisfy you and remove that rock (as you call it), which in your apprehensions is of so great danger, I am at last resolved to let you see that I value your affections for me at as high a rate as you yourself can set it, and that you cannot have more of tenderness for me and my interests than I shall ever have for yours. The particulars how I intend to make this good you shall know when I see you; which since I find them here more irresolute in point of time (though not as to the journey itself) than I hoped they would have been, notwithstanding your quarrel to me, and the apprehension you would make me believe you had that I do not care to see you, pray come hither and try whether you shall be welcome or not! In sober earnest now I must speak with you; and to that end if your occasions will give you leave as soon as you have received this come down to Canterbury. Send someone when you are there, and you shall have further directions.

You must be contented not to stay here above two to three hours. I shall tell you my reason when you come. And pray inform yourself of all that your father will do in this occasion, that you may tell it me only; therefore let it be plainly and sincerely what he intends and all.

I will not hinder your coming away so much as the making this letter a little longer might take away from your time in reading it. 'Tis enough to tell you I am ever

Yours.

* 'Spot' was a variety of pigeon, but the reference here may also be to a certain type of dog.

Epilogue

Here the letters end, but there are several sources providing us with details of the events of the months that followed Dorothy's arrival in London on October 17th, 1654. Henry Osborne's diary, Lady Giffard's Life of Sir William Temple, *and a few notes written by Dorothy herself complement each other and present a touchingly human account of three very trying months.*

After giving the reader a summary of her brother's relationship with Dorothy, Lady Giffard turns to the events of the autumn of 1654. 'But the misfortunes of this *amour* were not yet ended. The week before they were to be married she fell so desperately ill there was little hopes of her life, and nothing, the doctors said, but its proving the smallpox could have saved her. He [*Temple*] was happy when he saw that [*her life*] secure, his kindness having greater ties than that of her beauty, though that loss was too great to leave him wholly insensible. He saw her constantly while she was ill, and married her soon after.'

Henry Osborne's account is, naturally, more concerned with the necessity of concluding a suitable marriage settlement. On October 17th he records what sounds like a demand from Dorothy: 'My Lady Peyton and my sister came to London from Knowlton, Sir Thomas Peyton staying behind. I kept my chamber that day and they stopped at my lodging at Mr. Palin's and my sister came and stayed supper with me, and then declared she would marry Temple.'

Two of Dorothy's short notes to Temple were probably written soon after her arrival in London and before her attack of smallpox. They both suggest that she is happily confident of becoming Temple's wife, and their tone implies that a firmer obligation now exists between them:

I

You are like to have an excellent housewife of me, I am abed still and slept so soundly, nothing but your letter could have waked me. You shall hear from me as soon as we have dined.

Farewell! Can you endure that word? No, out upon't, I'll see you anon.

II

Fie upon't, I shall grow too good now! I am taking care to know how your worship slept tonight, better I hope than you did the last. Send me word how you do, and don't put me off with a bit of a note now; you could write me a fine long letter when I did not deserve it half so well.

Henry Osborne's diary records the fact that Dorothy fell ill with smallpox on November 9th, but contains no personal comment and betrays no emotion at all. On December 13th he returns to the subject of the marriage settlement: 'Sir John Temple came to Sir Thomas Hatton's about a treaty with my sister.' *(Hatton was one of the trustees of the estate of Sir Peter Osborne.) On December 22nd he writes:* 'I carried Sir Thomas Hatton Sir John Temple's draft for settling things upon marriage, with the corrections of Sir Orlando Bridgeman, which he seemed to consent to all but the £1500 that was to return to the family in case her issue failed, as he said; but he, in truth, would only meddle with the business of the £1000 and would have nothing to do with the other £3000, whereupon Sir Thomas Hatton told him that without he did one, we should not do the other, and that it was not in my sister's power to hinder it. Upon this, he quite flew off, and said he would do nothing, and so parted. The next day my sister told it me, and we utterly fell out about it.'

But despite this continued disagreement, the banns were read and Dorothy and William were married in the Parish Church of St Giles-in-the-Fields on Christmas Day, 1654. Henry's diary has an extraordinarily laconic entry: 'Being Christmas Day, my sister was married, and went as she said to Mr. Franklin's.'

Mrs Franklin was Dorothy's cousin and Mr Franklin was a friend of the Temple family. At their home at Moor Park in Hertfordshire, a place that Temple had always found most sympathetic, the lovers discovered the happiness of which they had both dreamed for so long. But Henry was not to leave them in peace. Despite Dorothy's sincere attempts to remain friends with her brother throughout the trying years, and her staunch defence of him in the final letters to Temple from Knowlton, Henry

204

behaved badly. He had always professed to love his sister, but it was a strange, possessive love, as many of the letters reveal. His diary records months and months of delay, scheming and deliberate misunderstanding on his part in arriving at a final settlement. A final agreement was only reached in July 1655 after the threat of even lengthier legal proceedings. Dorothy must have felt somewhat disillusioned about her brother, and his behaviour undoubtedly cast a shadow over the first months of her married life. But that may well have been his intention. Dorothy, however, did not let him ruin her happiness: there is little evidence of their meeting more than very occasionally after the summer of 1655.

From this time on the story of Dorothy's life must be sought in the career of her distinguished husband, and strictly speaking lies outside the scope of this book. In one sense it was a romantic story, but in another sense it was anything but the life that the romantic Dorothy had once envisaged in the early days of her friendship with Temple. She travelled with him and experienced the excitement of Continental diplomatic life; she became the intimate friend of royalty; she was at the centre of great events, and she became a patroness of the arts. But she never really knew the idyllic joy of a life of seclusion and contemplation, which at one time she had dreamed of attaining. Instead, she discovered that she had been right to doubt the possibility of finding perfect happiness in this life: she buried all nine of the children she bore Temple, seven of them in infancy, and throughout her married life she supported Temple faithfully and tirelessly in his duties, not always pleasant ones.

After reading Dorothy Osborne's letters to Temple one can only regret the fact that there are so few letters from Dorothy Temple to her husband William: the desire to know how she wrote to him after they were married is irresistible.

The three letters that follow are representative of her years of married life. The first was written when her first baby was nine months old; the second finds her discussing politics in a letter from The Hague, and the third was written to a nephew thanking him for his consolation on the death of her son in 1689.

In 1656 the Temples were living at Reading, having returned from a visit to Ireland. This letter can be dated quite reliably: the fair referred to is the St Matthew's Day Fair held in Reading on September 21st, 1656. Little Jack, now nine months old, has been invited to stay with Lady Vachell at Coley, her house near Reading:

My dearest heart,

After all Mr. Mayor's preparations, 'twas a very poor fair. Not a good horse in't Sawyer's team, in which was the mare he told you of, and he brought her down to the stable to match her with my aunt's, and they do very well together, he says. But I did not see it, for though I sent twenty messengers to him, Sadler would not come near me all the fair day, but sent me word at night what he had done, which was that on Saturday next here would come two mares for you to see. Today I sent for him again, and he tells me the mares are both Sawyer's, both 4 years old, and full as least as my aunt's and the same colour, and will both come to about £30, one of them he has been offered £16 for and he takes her to be better than my aunt's. There was but yet one here, but Sawyer tells him the other is full as good as my aunt's, and if you like them you may have them, if not there's no harm done, he is not fond of selling them. I have seen the young fellow: he looks plain and honest; will undertake, he says, to look to your 4 horses very well and with as much care as any man. Sadler commends him mightily. He drove his brother's coach the Gloucester road a great while. He asks £12 a year and cannot take under, he says; he had as much of Sadler's brother and has as good as £16 where he is now. Sadler and he go up together tomorrow; there you may see him and satisfy yourself. But with all this I must tell you too that they say Sadler is generally taken notice on for a gift he has in lying, and therefore what his mares will come to I cannot tell. Can you tell me when you intend to come home? Would you would, I should take it mighty kindly. Good dear, make haste, I am as weary as a dog without you. Poor Jack is all the entertainment I have. He mems his little duty and grows and thrives every day. When the sun shines his maid has him abroad to use him to the air against his journey, and he is shortly to go to Coley upon a solemn invitation. My dear heart, be sure I have a scrip by Tuesday's coach, and no reproaches, remember that; indeed, I don't deserve them I think, for I'm sure I infinitely love my dearest dear heart, and am his.

D. Temple.

If you can conveniently, I should be glad you paid the Grocer's bill.

The second letter was written in 1670, when Temple was ambassador at The Hague. He returned to England on duty, leaving Dorothy behind in Holland. She reveals remarkable knowledge of contemporary affairs, showing the extent to which she had identified herself with her husband's profession.

My dearest heart, I received yours from Yarmouth, and was very glad you made so happy a passage. 'Tis a comfortable thing, when one is on this side, to know that such a thing can be done in spite of contrary winds. I have a letter from P., who says in character that you may take it from him that the Duke of Buckingham has begun a negotiation there, but what success he may have in England he knows not; that it were to be wished our politicians at home would consider well that there is no trust to be put in alliances with ambitious kings, especially such as make it their fundamental maxim to be base. These are bold words, but they are his own. Besides this, there is nothing but that the French King grows very thrifty, that all his buildings, except fortifications, are ceased, and that his payments are not so regular as they used to be. The people here are of another mind; they will not spare their money, but are resolved—at least the States of Holland, if the rest will consent—to raise fourteen new regiments of foot and six troops of horse; that all the companies, both old and new, shall be of 120 men that used to be of 50, and every troop 80 that used to be of 45. Nothing is talked of but these new levies, and the young men are much pleased. Downton says they have strong suspicions here you will come back no more, and that they shall be left in the lurch; that something is striking up with France, and that you are sent away because you are too well inclined to these countries; and my cousin Temple, he says, told him that a nephew of Sir Robert Long's, who is lately come to Utrecht, told my cousin Temple, three weeks since, you were not to stay long here, because you were too great a friend to these people, and that they had it from Mr. Williamson, who knew very well what he said. My cousin Temple says he told it Major Scott as soon as he heard it, and so 'tis like you knew it before; but here is such want of something to say that I catch at everything. I am my best dear's most affectionate

D. T.

The third letter was not written to Temple. It was to her nephew Sir John Osborne, who had written to her to console her on the tragic death of her only surviving child, John. He had drowned himself.

SHEEN, MAY 6TH, 1689

Dear Nephew, I give you many thanks for your kind letter and the sense you have of my affliction, which truly is very great. But since it is laid upon me by the hand of an Almighty and Gracious God, that always proportions His punishments to the support He gives with them, I may hope to bear it as a Christian ought to do, and more especially one that is conscious to herself of having many ways deserved it. The strange revolutions we have seen might well have taught me what this world is, yet it seems it was necessary that I should have a near example of the uncertainty of all human blessings, that so having no tie to the world, I may the better prepare myself to leave it; and that this correction may suffice to teach me my duty must be the prayer of your affectionate aunt and humble servant,

D. Temple.

Dorothy died in February 1695, four years before her husband. His young protégé, Jonathan Swift, characterized her as 'mild Dorothea, peaceful, wise and great.' All those who have enjoyed the experience of reading her letters will certainly accept this as her most fitting epitaph.

Index of Proper Names